HIDDEN
HISTORY
of
GAMECOCKS
FOOTBALL

HIDDEN
HISTORY
of
GAMECOCKS
FOOTBALL

David Caraviello

THE
History
PRESS

Published by The History Press
Charleston, SC
www.historypress.com

Copyright © 2020 by David Caraviello
All rights reserved

Front cover: Russell Maxey Photograph Collection, courtesy of Richland Library, Columbia, S.C
Back cover, top: The State Newspaper Photograph Archive, courtesy of Richland Library, Columbia, S.C.; *bottom*: The State Newspaper Photograph Archive, courtesy of Richland Library, Columbia, S.C

First published 2020

Manufactured in the United States

ISBN 9781467143318

Library of Congress Control Number: 2020938436

For Sarah and Declan

CONTENTS

PREFACE

The University of South Carolina Gamecocks began playing football in 1892 and since then have become as much a part of the Palmetto State's fiber as shrimp boats, boiled peanuts and humidity. Another certain state school has enjoyed periods of greater on-field success, but from the Sea Islands to the Appalachian foothills, the Gamecocks have always been the larger presence. South Carolina is the bigger school with the larger enrollment, with double the number of living alumni compared to its Upstate rival. If you live and work within the confines of this little pie-shaped state, the gridiron struggles and successes of the state's flagship university are plainly evident all around.

And goodness, what a roller-coaster ride it's been. An out-of-nowhere breakthrough in 1984, which had the Gamecocks on the cusp of the national championship game, scuttled by an unthinkable loss to a Navy team that would go 4-6-1. An unparalleled assemblage of talent in 1987 that appeared to set South Carolina on the right track for years to come, derailed the following season by a scandal and the death of its head coach. Consecutive 1-10 and 0-11 seasons that had the program wandering in the wilderness as never before. The unprecedented success coinciding with the arrival of Steve Spurrier, who beat Clemson five straight times and won eleven games three years in a row before recruiting shortcomings again sent the Gamecocks tumbling into mediocrity.

It's a long-running saga that's become well known to just about anyone who grew up a sports fan in South Carolina. It's certainly been that way for me, someone born and raised in the Palmetto State, who attended the University of South Carolina, twice covered the Gamecocks as a newspaper beat writer and ascended that elevator to the press box level at Williams-Brice Stadium more times than I can count. The first came in mid-September 1988, when the press box was on the club level between the two decks on the stadium's west side. It was open-air, so the heat and noise and atmosphere could all come flooding in. Joe Morrison was in his final season as head coach, and the program was weeks away from the publication of a *Sports Illustrated* exposé that would allege widespread steroid use in the Gamecocks locker room. But on that Saturday in 1988, before a victory over East Carolina, few had an inkling of the tumult to come.

The press box had yet to be moved to a much more spacious and well-appointed facility perched atop the west stand's upper deck. There were only low-rise seats behind either end zone; the football office building, topped by its updated scoreboard, had yet to be built on one end; and "The Zone" suite area and its accompanying upper deck were still years away from reality on the other. The area surrounding the stadium was a wasteland of boxy commercial buildings bordered by the ramshackle state farmers market, giving no indication of the lush, landscaped tailgating areas yet to come. Many of South Carolina's facilities were behind the times, a vestige of years as an independent, but that fact that didn't truly hit home until four years later when the Gamecocks joined the SEC. Morrison could only have dreamed of a practice complex such as the one South Carolina completed in 2019, complete with a one-hundred-yard indoor facility and a $50 million operations center.

For those who remember how things used to be, the physical transformation of South Carolina's football program has been stunning, with the Gamecocks benefiting from some amenities that even more successful SEC rivals have yet to construct. With its adjacent tailgate areas and surrounding plaza, Williams-Brice now looks like part of the main campus rather than this far outpost where the football team operates. After years of having coaches' offices located in one place, strength and conditioning facilities based in another and practice fields situated across a four-lane highway—which had to be blocked twice a day by university police so players could safely navigate it—everything is consolidated in one area. The Gamecocks have never been better equipped to succeed.

Oh, but then there's that not-so-small matter of performance on the field, which South Carolina throughout its history has been able to sustain only in fits and starts, never long enough for the program to build the kind of internal momentum that sustains elite teams through years and decades of on-field success. In fact, real success in football has been only a fairly recent development at South Carolina, which remained under .500 for much of its history. Things didn't truly turn around until the arrival of Lou Holtz, who pulled the Gamecocks out of their miserable 0-11 doldrums from 1999 with a pair of Outback Bowl victories over Ohio State that offered a real taste of sustained accomplishment. Over the following nineteen years, the Gamecocks finished with winning or break-even records fifteen times. By South Carolina standards, that's a major upgrade in performance, and it comes with raised expectations. Will Muschamp, hired as head coach in late 2015, knows that well—he heard plenty of grief from fans following an ugly bowl loss to complete the 2018 season and even more during a 4-8 disappointment the following year.

So, there's a colorful, somewhat star-crossed history to the South Carolina football program, one that's familiar to anyone who wears a Gamecocks logo on their golf shirt or came up reading the works of great Palmetto State sports columnists like Ken Burger, Bob Gillespie or Dan Foster in their local newspaper. And yet there's so much that remains little known, whether it's untold stories about seasons or happenings from the first half of the twentieth century or smaller, hidden facets to events that many people otherwise know very well. What really happened in the riot after the Clemson game in 1902? Why was football banned at South Carolina for one season? How did a multimillion-dollar gift to the university end up funding the expansion of Williams-Brice Stadium? How did quarterback Connor Shaw really feel in the days leading up to the "Miracle at Missouri" game in 2013? What really led to the hiring of Muschamp as South Carolina's head coach?

Other events, some of them major—such as South Carolina's handling of the aftermath of President John F. Kennedy's assassination, the impact of World War II on the program or even the steroid scandal of 1988—have seen their impact or their notoriety dulled by the passage of time. Those are the stories this book hopes to tell: the ones that have been forgotten or overlooked or that turned out to be small but important elements of something much bigger. Even as someone who spent two stints writing about the Gamecocks; sat though innumerable press conferences, games and player interviews; and covered a handful of firings and subsequent coaching searches, I learned so much by going deep into the archives and dusting off buried bits of South Carolina football history from the early 1900s to the modern age. Hopefully, you'll enjoy the results.

ACKNOWLEDGEMENTS

When editor Chad Rhoad from The History Press first contacted me about writing this, I was hesitant—despite an extensive career in journalism, the longest piece I'd ever written was roughly ten thousand words. A book would be roughly four times longer than that. Faced with the prospect of long hours zipping back and forth through reels of microfilm, the intimidation was genuine. But the research turned out to be among the most enjoyable professional endeavors I've ever undertaken, thanks to how easy the Charleston County Library and Richland Library made it.

So, thanks begin with the staffs at the Charleston and Columbia libraries and their extensive online collections of their respective local newspapers dating back to the late 1800s. It was a thrill to be sitting at my desk in Charleston, flipping through pages of *The State* from 1902. Without digitized versions of both newspapers being so readily available to library members through the online NewsBank portal, the research for this project would have been pure drudgery. Instead, easy-to-find details from every era helped provide the book with a broad context and made the players, coaches and other figures truly come alive.

Thanks also to Chad for his patience as a first-time author tried to manage research and writing amid myriad other freelance projects and two small children who needed baths and bedtime. Thanks to Ben Johansen, who gave an early draft of the book a needed proofread while at 35,000 feet somewhere above the Atlantic Ocean. Thanks to former South Carolina sports information director Kerry Tharp, who helped me come up with a rough listing of what subjects needed to be covered. Thanks to colleague David Cloninger, who provided phone numbers for some key sources. And thanks to friend, colleague and mentor Gene Sapakoff for recommending that, whenever possible, the book take on a narrative style that would help the stories jump off the page.

Managing the research and writing was one thing; finding the necessary photos for the book was quite another. In that area, my undisputed hero and saving grace was Margaret Dunlap of Richland Library's Walker Local and Family History Center. She went above and beyond to help me acquire roughly two dozen images, the majority of them from the photo archives of *The State* newspaper housed at the library. Some had never been seen in print before—she pulled them from decades-old reels of thirty-five-millimeter film. Margaret was as important to getting this project completed as anyone, and I owe her an immense debt of thanks.

Another huge thank-you goes to Liz Foster at the *Post and Courier* newspaper in Charleston, who went above and beyond in record time to help find the final few images needed for the book as deadline approached. Thanks also to Tracy Glantz, who helped me acquire the necessary permissions to use *The State* photos; to McKenzie Lemhouse of the Caroliniana Library at the University of South Carolina, who helped locate archival images from the early 1900s; Gamecocks sports information director Steve Fink; and Heather Moore of the U.S. Senate Historical Office, who found me photos of state legislators. The Library of Congress, John F. Kennedy Presidential Library and Theodore Roosevelt Center were also helpful in supplying images.

Tommy Suggs, Steve Taneyhill, Connor Shaw, Brad Edwards, Travis Haney, David Newton, Ryan Wood and Bob Gillespie were among those who were extremely gracious in spending time sharing their memories. Photographers Allen Sharpe and Jenny Dilworth proved key in helping me locate Margaret Dunlap at Richland Library. And a huge debt of thanks to my wife, Katie Brennan, who encouraged me to take on this project despite my initial hesitancies—it proved to be incredibly rewarding. She's my better half for a reason.

—David Caraviello
Charleston, South Carolina
August 30, 2019

1

A Riotous Mood

Christie Benet Jr. stood atop the low brick wall that surrounded the Horseshoe and assessed a deteriorating situation that was growing more dangerous by the minute. On one side, there were by his estimation three hundred military cadets from what was then called Clemson Agricultural College, all of them angry and all of them armed. On the other, there were roughly sixty students of what at the time was known as South Carolina College, and they were dug in with clubs, pistols and whatever other weapons they had scrounged in defense of their campus.

Within that latter group was sophomore James Rion McKissick, a future president of the University of South Carolina. He felt a hand on his shoulder. "Are you armed?" an upperclassman asked him. McKissick flashed a glimpse of his revolver. "Make every shot count!" he was told.

Tempers were flaring, tension was high and the potential for bloodshed was in the air. All of it was over college football, which has inflamed passions around the Palmetto State in the decades since, but perhaps never more than at the gates of the Horseshoe on Halloween night in 1902, when South Carolina's second-ever victory over its blossoming Upstate rival led to a tense, armed confrontation at the entrance to its central campus. It took the quick thinking of a young Gamecocks assistant coach to maintain a tenuous hold on order—and prevent potential loss of life—before Columbia police finally intervened.

Up on the Horseshoe wall, Benet could sense a grim culmination to the friction that had been evident in Columbia all week, leaving nerves frayed to their very edges. A scrape on the evening following the annual Big Thursday game at the state fairgrounds, a 12–6 victory by the Gamecocks, had reportedly involved the use of brass knuckles by South Carolina students and the unsheathing of swords by Clemson cadets. From his perch, Benet could see that the cadets now had their bayonets drawn. Desperate to do anything to prevent the outbreak of violence, he offered to represent all of the South Carolina students in fighting whomever the cadets chose to represent the Clemson side, hoping to settle the issue one-on-one.

"There was no acceptance," Benet later wrote, as the atmosphere grew more grim.

It was all a stark contrast to the merriment of the previous morning, when the budding rivalry game brought out all the pomp and circumstance that the fledgling sport of college football could muster. There was a parade of carriages bearing the names of sponsors, there were beautiful women waving to the crowd, there were greats of South Carolina's brief football past in attendance. And the final result evidently wasn't as close as the six-point margin might indicate. "The way Carolina's ends and tackles shot through Clemson's men and hit her players…was something to make any Carolina heart glad," read one report from the scene. "It showed football training and football skill. Clemson tried every trick play in their catalogue and failed utterly at all of them."

The result was robustly celebrated by Carolina supporters, and understandably so, given that it represented South Carolina's second victory ever over its in-state rival and snapped a four-game skid stretching back to the inaugural contest between the two teams in 1896. Members of the South Carolina student body jubilantly sang "We'll Twist the Tiger's Tail" from the sideline, and reports indicate no animosity during the game—despite the fights between students that marred much of the week. Clemson, coached at the time by John Heisman, "took the defeat in good grace," the game report reads. "In fact, it is a rare thing that one sees men act in the true spirit of sport that the Clemson boys did."

For the fledgling state college, though, the victory brought a needed dose of confidence, both from an athletic and a campus-wide perspective. The early losing streak to Clemson was evidence of how ramshackle the birth of South Carolina's football program had been—the college was late in forming a team compared to many other schools in the region, and the team's first game a decade earlier against Furman had been a slapdash affair, held not in Columbia but in Charleston, with South Carolina having no head coach and two nonstudents on the roster. Players had to pay for their own transportation to the game. With the team having no nickname, the Charleston paper simply referred to the South Carolina side as "the College Boys." So, it was no surprise that Furman won easily, 44–0.

Administrators at South Carolina College had yielded to allow athletics during a time of cutbacks and purse-tightening, doing so not in some pursuit of on-field glory but in the hope that students would pursue an outlet for "expressing high spirits in a form less destructive to property," Daniel Walker Hollis wrote in his definitive two-volume history of the university. For the school that would one day become a sprawling city unto itself, these were lean years. There was only one telephone on campus, in a law-enforcement office that students complained was always locked. The college's president was lobbying state lawmakers for the installation of sewage facilities that would connect to a citywide system in the midst of being built. Electricity was coming, but slowly, with dormitories and professors' houses being wired first.

Things hadn't always been so austere. South Carolina College at the turn of the twentieth century, Hollis wrote, was a shadow of its former self, due in large part to budget cuts enacted by Governor Ben Tillman, who oversaw the state from 1890 to 1894 and whose name would become nearly synonymous with another school. Instrumental in the founding of Clemson, Tillman was an ardent believer in decentralized higher education, as opposed to a single, grand university. "The founding of Clemson, born in social upheaval and political strife…was designed not only to help the poor farmer's son get an education, but, many would agree, to also help disembowel the University of South Carolina," Robert A. Pierce, former associate editor of Columbia's *The State* newspaper, wrote in the year of Clemson's 100th birthday.

So, there was acrimony, right from the start, with South Carolina College viewing this agricultural school in a small Upstate town as a threat to its very existence as budgets were slashed and enrollment fell at the flagship university in Columbia. "At the turn of the century the College needed, more than anything else," Hollis wrote, "a sense of continuity, for the sake of both public and self-confidence."

A notable football victory helped. By 1902, football had become the top sport on campus, a position it has enjoyed for most of the university's history since. So, losses to Clemson irked in more ways than one, especially given that cadets would celebrate their victories by parading through Columbia with their shoes wrapped in garnet and black cloth. A Columbia tobacco store, decorated with displays for both teams prior to the big game, offered the perfect antidote: an illustration drawn by a South Carolina College

Scene from a South Carolina football game against Clemson in the first decade of the twentieth century. The Tigers dominated the Gamecocks early in the series, winning five of the first seven games in the rivalry. *Courtesy of South Caroliniana Library, University of South Carolina, Columbia, S.C.*

mathematics professor named F. Horton Colcock. The drawing was a "transparency," a type of artwork popularly used for decoration in the nineteenth century, done on a translucent substance such as silk or linen cloth and illuminated from behind for effect. The transparency in the tobacco store showed a crowing, victorious gamecock adorned with an "S.C.C." The fighting rooster was standing over a dead tiger.

South Carolina students had their celebratory emblem, and they planned to carry it in the Elks Club parade the day following the game. By modern standards, the illustration is innocuous, akin to those now seen on bumper stickers adorning thousands of cars in the Palmetto State. But in 1902, it tossed gasoline atop what was already a flammable brew. And it was how Christie Benet Jr. found himself standing on top of a wall encircling the Horseshoe, trying to stop two groups of students from killing each other.

If there was anyone who had the clout on both sides to pull it off, it was Benet, who had been a standout player at both Virginia and South Carolina and served as an assistant coach in Columbia while also working as an attorney. During his playing days, the former halfback and lineman showed "remarkable ability in carrying the ball" and was "a tackler of no [average] ability," the *Charleston Evening Post* wrote of Benet. More important, given the situation, was the fact that Benet's father, a former state senator, had sponsored a bill that helped establish Clemson as a college and later served as a Clemson trustee.

So, when Clemson's commandant of cadets wanted to speak with someone about the transparency South Carolina students planned to carry in the parade, it was Benet who was summoned. Benet's account is detailed in an extensive letter to *The State* newspaper, correcting what he viewed as "somewhat incomplete" initial reporting that underplayed the menacing nature of the incident. Mounted on horseback, former U.S. Army cavalryman and Clemson commandant E.A. Sirmyer told Benet that his cadets would view the transparency as an insult. The arrogance was too much for Benet, well aware of how cadets had boasted during a scrape the previous day that they would not allow South Carolina students to carry the illustration in the parade. He refused Sirmyer's request to leave it behind.

The propensity for violence then truly began to stir. "We'll take it," Benet claims a Clemson cadet told Sirmyer, in the presence of the South Carolina assistant coach. "I know you will," the commandant allegedly responded. Benet was dumbfounded and asked whether Sirmyer could control his men. The commandant offered a chilling response: "I will not be responsible."

As the parade passed the agricultural hall that served as Clemson's headquarters in Columbia, a rock was thrown and struck the carriage in which the transparency was being carried. The remainder of the parade passed without incident, and it would have been natural for Benet to believe the danger had passed. He made a short speech to the South Carolina students before they dispersed. "Carolina had carried her point," he said, urging them to "be careful to avoid any trouble that night."

But trouble would find them. Benet was walking back from the parade when some South Carolina students met him at the intersection of Sumter and Pendleton Streets and told him that armed Clemson cadets were coming in force. A few dozen South Carolina students assembled behind the Horseshoe wall; the cadets "stopped at the end of the sidewalk, drawn up in close formation parallel with the wall, numbering 300 and 400," Benet wrote, "and all appeared with their side arms." The cadets were in "a riotous mood," he added.

His gambit to settle the matter by fighting one member of the Clemson entourage having failed, Benet proposed arbitration, with committees of three men on each side chosen to settle the matter. By this time, Benet could see Columbia's police chief walking amid the cadets trying to calm tensions.

A squad of police would arrive soon after. The chances of an outbreak of violence, it seemed, were dropping by the minute. The proposal to form three-man committees was accepted, and both sides agreed that their decisions would be binding. Clemson cadets demanded that Benet apologize to Sirmyer in person for assuming his words conveyed a threat, which the South Carolina assistant coach agreed to do. The members of both committees then came to the conclusion that the transparency should be burned.

Among the South Carolina students, there was rancor over the decision, which was initially seen as a capitulation to the Clemson cadets. Benet then found himself trying to cool tensions among members of his own side, reminding them that everyone had agreed that the decision of the committees would be binding. "Finally, they relented," Benet wrote. The illustration, which had inflamed so many passions, met its own demise in flame. The crowd dispersed. Conflict had been avoided, and no one had been hurt. It had been less a riot than an armed standoff, one in which weapons had been brandished but not used. The episode was, thankfully, over.

Except, of course, it wasn't. Once reports of that night became widespread, Clemson claimed the whole saga was overblown, with former football coach and future school president Walter M. Riggs calling it "a stir being made over what really amounted to nothing." There were charges in the Upstate that the whole thing was blown out of proportion by the local paper. In Columbia, though, where many recalled seeing Clemson cadets brandish bayonets and swords, the incident was taken much more seriously. So much so that lingering tension between the two schools over the near-riot led South Carolina's faculty committee on athletics to cancel the series between the in-state rivals. It would remain idle until it was resumed in 1909.

The thaw began in 1908, when Davidson played South Carolina and Clemson on consecutive days in Columbia. Members of the South Carolina student body invited Clemson players to a meeting at the university's chapel, where the two sides began the discussions that would put the unpleasantness of 1902 behind them. "The old chapel was decorated in both purple-and-orange and garnet-and-black for the occasion," Hollis wrote. Speeches of conciliation were made by representatives of both parties, and Hollis wrote that "the students cemented the peace pact by joining in a parade to serenade the girls at the College for Women." From there, negotiations to resume the series in 1909 commenced.

But that early chapter in South Carolina football history had ramifications that remain evident even today, in the Gamecocks mascot that's become synonymous with the athletic department. In a graduate paper written on the

Before he became president of the University of South Carolina in 1936, James Rion McKissick was a sophomore at South Carolina College involved in the 1902 standoff with Clemson cadets. *Courtesy of South Caroliniana Library, University of South Carolina, Columbia, S.C.*

episode, author Jacob McCormick argues that the transparency that sparked tensions in 1902 led to the adoption of the Gamecock as the university's symbol, as well the formation of the school's first athletic booster clubs. The first reference to "Game Cocks" in relation to South Carolina football was used in *The State* newspaper in 1903. The term itself is widely believed to have originated with the nickname of Revolutionary War general Thomas Sumter—also the namesake of Fort Sumter in Charleston Harbor—who became known as "The Fighting Gamecock" for his tenacious efforts in preventing the Redcoats from gaining a foothold in South Carolina.

Benet, meanwhile, continued to play a role with the program, serving four years as head coach until stepping down to devote more time to his law practice. He briefly served in the U.S. Senate, completing the remainder of a term left when Tillman—ironically, the former governor who was South Carolina's nemesis from the turn of the century—died in office in 1918. But at the University of South Carolina, nothing can approach his actions on the night of October 31, 1902, when he stood atop a wall between two groups of armed men and kept near-certain bloodshed at bay.

2

BANNED

The president of the University of South Carolina walked out of the campus library to face hundreds of students who had gathered outside. In the crowd, hope mingled with anxiety over the future of the university's intercollegiate football program, which had rapidly become the most popular sports team on campus. But at the moment, South Carolina didn't have a football program at all—the squad had been disbanded as part of a national movement to ban the sport. There had been too many catastrophic injuries and too many deaths. Too many universities had seen enough. Across America, one school after another began to drop football. South Carolina was one of them.

The student body, though, was determined to see football return. Students had attempted once before to get the football program reinstated, petitioning the board of trustees the previous spring, only to have their request denied. Now they were back again, and in larger numbers, with another petition in the fall of 1907, when universities around the country were in the midst of a new football season played under a new set of rules implemented to try and make the game safer. Meanwhile, the South Carolina squad sat idle, its playing field unused—all of this at a university that in a very short time had developed a fervent passion for the sport.

The students had timed their latest request impeccably, to coincide with State Fair week, when South Carolina traditionally played in-state rival Clemson. The Tigers were still there in Columbia, but to play North Carolina at the fairgrounds rather than at South Carolina, and among

University of South Carolina president Benjamin Sloan was a staunch supporter of the school's football program, even after it was banned by the board of trustees as part of a nationwide movement against an increasingly violent sport. *Courtesy of South Caroliniana Library, University of South Carolina, Columbia, S.C.*

Gamecocks faithful, the absence of the home team was glaring on the sport's biggest week in the Palmetto State. But the board of trustees had its concerns—not just about fatalities (understandable given the coast-to-coast bloodshed the game caused in the early 1900s), but also about lawsuits and players spending too much time away from school.

So, when President Benjamin Sloan emerged from the fall board of trustees meeting at the university library, there was no way of knowing what message he carried with him. He faced the assembled crowd and told the students that their petition had been granted. Initially, there was a brief silence as the news sunk in.

"Then a mighty yell rent the air," *The State* newspaper reported.

It marked the end to a contentious period, one that had begun in January 1906, when the board of trustees had acted on a suggestion by member R.P. Hamer Jr. that the university ban intercollegiate football. The motion came as the Gamecocks program had at last built some real momentum, reeling off four straight winning seasons for the first time in its brief history, the two most recent coming under head coach Christie Benet Jr.—the same man who had helped prevent bloodshed between armed groups of Clemson and South Carolina students four years earlier.

But the victories overshadowed problems off the field. The Gamecocks had faced one eligibility issue after another, author Daniel Walker Hollis wrote in his two-volume history of the university. At one point, South Carolina was blacklisted by the Southern Intercollegiate Athletic Association—the forerunner to the modern Southern Conference—for using an ineligible player in a 1903 game against Georgia Tech. The Faculty Athletic Committee, which oversaw the program, found football increasingly difficult to control and ultimately developed a fundamental disdain for intercollegiate athletics as a whole.

"High ideals are regarded as incongruous with the very spirit of athletics," the faculty committee wrote in a special report to the board of trustees, as told by Hollis, and scruples were "mere prudishness." The report suggested "the abominable habit of rooting should be discouraged. Men who cannot win athletic contests without the aid of brass horns, bass drums, and brazen lungs should be deported to China to serve in the army of that empire."

South Carolina's board of trustees began investigating alleged impropriety within the football program in 1904, initially appointing a committee of three professors, two alumni and two students to direct intercollegiate athletics—essentially removing the faculty from its oversight position, given that it could always be outvoted. And then came 1905, the deadliest year in college football history, which prompted colleges nationwide to drop the game and took presidential intervention to save it.

Football had become less of a game than a blood sport, and opposition to it was understandable given the carnage. At the turn of the twentieth century, there was little structure—teams often negotiated rules between themselves. It was a brute-force game with no quarterbacks or receivers, in which the participants wore little or no protective gear (even leather helmets would not become standard for another three decades) and piles of large men jabbed, kicked and punched at one another. A *New York Times* report of a game between Columbia and Yale in the 1890s detailed one player taking a shot to the knee, another kicked in the abdomen and another struck so hard in the ribs he had to be carried off the field. Cracked bones and concussions were "generally accepted as the unfortunate by-products of a demanding and entertaining sport," author John J. Miller wrote of the era.

But what galvanized national attention were the deaths. In 1905, at least 18 people died from playing football, and more than 150 had been injured in that same year. According to the *Washington Post*, at least 45 football players died between 1900 and 1905. There was no artistry or elegance to the game: with forward passes illegal and only five yards needed for a

Serious injuries and even deaths became commonplace across college football in the early twentieth century. The problem caught the attention of President Theodore Roosevelt after his son Theodore Jr. (*center*) was injured playing at Harvard. *Courtesy of Library of Congress Prints and Photographs Division, Theodore Roosevelt Digital Library, Dickinson State University.*

first down, contests consisted of short, lateral tosses and masses of players colliding with one another—some suffering broken backs, broken necks or internal injuries in the process. "Picked up unconscious from beneath a mass of other players, it was generally found that the victim had been kicked in the head or stomach, so as to cause internal injuries or concussion of the brain, which, sooner or later, ended life," the *Washington Post* wrote in 1905.

Some instances were especially gruesome and made national headlines. An 1894 game between Harvard and Yale became known as the "Hampden Park Blood Bath" because of its brutality and prompted Harvard president Charles Eliot to call for the sport's abolishment. And in 1905, Union College halfback Harold Moore died of a cerebral hemorrhage after being kicked in the head while making a tackle against New York University. An editorial cartoon in the *Cincinnati Commercial Tribune* showed a scythe-carrying Grim Reaper sitting atop a goal post, the tangled bodies of football players lying on the turf before him, the whole scene looking more like a war zone than a field of play. The crisis even attracted the attention of President Theodore Roosevelt after his son suffered a serious cut over his eye playing for the Harvard freshman team. The *New York Times* fretted over the game's trend toward "mayhem and homicide" and ran an editorial headlined "Two Curable Evils"—referring to the lynching of African Americans and football.

And yet, it all made the game irresistible to onlookers, who had never seen anything like it. "Spectators enjoyed the clash of teams, the hard tackles, and the grit that players had to display as they shook off blows and ignored bruises," Miller wrote. On many college campuses, including South Carolina's, the game's popularity mushroomed, eclipsing that of any other athletic pursuit on campus. But many administrators felt otherwise; Harvard's Eliot in particular was a vocal crusader against the game, writing in 1905 that it embraced "the barbarous ethics of warfare." Others were clearly in agreement: Columbia, Stanford, Wake Forest, Duke (then known as Trinity), Northwestern, California, Brigham Young, Union College and other schools dropped their football programs amid public outcry over how dangerous the game had become.

It was in this atmosphere that the South Carolina board of trustees met in January 1906, already weary of the other issues stemming from friction between the football program and the faculty. Circumventing the seven-member board it had put in place to oversee the program a year earlier, the board in a six-hour meeting decided to follow the lead of other universities and drop football, stunning a campus that appeared to not anticipate the move.

There was no opportunity to argue otherwise. "This action was taken without reference to any outside influence or request," *The State* newspaper wrote at the time. Hamer, "who pressed the suggestion, thought that this was the very best time for the college to take this stand against football," the report continued. South Carolina had suffered no fatalities in its football program, and it had not been subjected to any outside legal action. After years of suffering under budget cutting from the state general assembly, the university was beginning to turn the corner financially, and there was no need to jeopardize it.

The surprise decision left students and supporters stunned and crestfallen. Students still got extra days off during State Fair week, as always, but now they didn't have a game to attend over the long weekend. In the football seasons to come, the local newspaper would run one story after another about college football—the big games that week, how other teams in the region were faring—and many were sure to include a mention of how South Carolina's once-strong program had been shuttered. "It is a source of much regret that the trustees did not deem it advisable to reinstate football at the university," *The State* bemoaned in the fall of 1907, "for Carolina no doubt would have had a strong eleven."

Amid the teeth-gnashing in Columbia, there were national efforts to modernize—and, in the process, save—what by that time had already become the favorite intercollegiate sport on many campuses. College football had no bigger advocate than Roosevelt, long a proponent of rugged physical exertion as key to a full, virile life. "We cannot afford to turn out college men who shrink from physical effort or from physical pain," the president said in a speech given at Harvard, as reported in (of course) *The State*. "Athletics are good, especially in their rougher forms, as they tend to develop such courage."

The Rough Rider took action, summoning football coaches from Harvard, Yale and Princeton to the White House for a summit on what do about the game. "Football is on trial," the president told those assembled. "Because I believe in the game, I want to do all I can to save it." There were camps with starkly different opinions. Some coaches understood the need for the sport's rules to be modernized; others were hesitant to change because their programs were thriving amid the chaos. Roosevelt, who in the aftermath of the Panama Canal compromise had earned a reputation as an effective negotiator, worked his charms. At his urging, representatives of sixty-two colleges and universities met in December 1905 to appoint a committee that would reexamine the rules of intercollegiate football. Three months later, the Intercollegiate Athletic Association of the United States—the body that would later evolve into the NCAA—was established to reform the game.

The changes resulted in a sport much closer to the one we see today: 10 yards rather than 5 necessary for a first down; legal forward passing; and a neutral zone established between the offensive and defensive lines. No surprise, *The State* in its pages trumpeted the rules changes as revolutionary. "Owing to a considerable extent the changes in the rules, the game has been more in favor with the public than heretofore," it wrote, in a thinly veiled message to the University of South Carolina board of trustees. "There are now more safeguards placed around the game and the rules give the officials increased powers that tend to eliminate all foul play." The result was "less severe pounding, more strategy, and…generally a far more open character" that "made way for the lighter, more active and aggressive dodger."

Within the university, the groundswell of support grew. Mathematics professor F.H. Colcock—the same educator who had designed the Gamecock transparency that caused all the trouble with Clemson back in 1902—wrote a defense of football in the university magazine. In the fall of 1907, the student body resubmitted its petition that the board reinstate football. The students had an ally in Sloan, the university president, a fan himself. "Supporters…have been very hopeful that the authorities would consent to restore the game," *The State* reported. "Football was the game in which the students took the most interest in, and the actions of the board came as a hard blow, especially to those who were in college at the time when the team of the South Carolina College was feared by other universities."

In the board's fall 1907 meeting, trustee Julius H. Walker introduced the resolution that students once again be able to compete in intercollegiate football. "The Board thought that the time [was] ripe for the restoration of football, [with] the sentiment in favor of restoring the game…growing for some time," *The State* reported. The rules changes had not solved every problem; there had still been eleven deaths in each of the 1906 and 1907 seasons, according to the *Washington Post*. But at South Carolina, the national reforms combined with the growing local pressure led the board to relent. After all of a 1906 season and most of a 1907 campaign without football, trustees approved Walker's motion to reinstate the game.

There was no shortage of celebration over football's return. The sport's reinstatement at South Carolina, and the refusal of a million-dollar endowment by Swarthmore College in Pennsylvania—offered with the stipulation that the school abolish athletics—were viewed regionally as examples of a sea change in opinion over the game. *The State* called them "significant symptoms of the popular reversal of sentiment in respect to the game of football as it is now revised, modified and improved."

Sloan, the university's president, was pleased as well. "As I am a firm believer in the value of athletic sport, I think the board has acted wisely," he told *The State* after informing the student body of the decision. Keenly aware of the role the local newspaper had played in pressuring the board of trustees to reverse its decision, the students paraded down to Main Street to offer three cheers for *The State*. Plans were immediately put in place to salvage something of what remained of the 1907 season, with the call going out for potential players to assemble at once. The result was a slate of three games all played in November, victories over College of Charleston, Georgia College and the Citadel by a combined score of 30–4—still the only unbeaten season in Gamecocks history.

3
VICTORY AND WAR

He was the first truly great player produced by the University of South Carolina football program, but Lou Sossamon's primary method of transportation remained his thumb. When traveling from Columbia back home to Gaffney, he caught rides by hitchhiking, a common practice of the day. So it was over the radio in the cab of a stranger's pickup truck that Sossamon heard the news that would alter the lives of so many young American men, his included: the Japanese had bombed Pearl Harbor in Hawaii, the act of aggression that would spur the United States to become involved in World War II.

Just six weeks earlier, his focus had been in a very different place. Sossamon had been a part of the biggest victory in South Carolina football history to that point—a stunner over Clemson that snapped a seven-game skid to their rivals, still the Gamecocks' longest losing streak in the series. And the opportunity was there for more, given that after suffering through two consecutive losing seasons, South Carolina had finished at break-even and had a roster of standout players coming back. The 1942 campaign had the potential to be one of the program's best, perhaps even the season where the Gamecocks turned the corner.

But suddenly, football's importance paled in comparison to the events happening in the wider world, brought home by stunning photos of battleships burning or sunken off the Hawaiian island of Oahu. The day that would live in infamy would scatter members of the South Carolina football squad across the globe, decimate a once-promising program for the following season and put any gridiron progress on indefinite hold.

"I have no idea who will be available when September comes," Gamecocks head coach Rex Enright told the local paper as he began piecing together a roster in the summer of 1942. "We are waiting for Uncle Sam to choose his side first, and we will take what is left."

What a contrast it was to the heady days of the previous season, capped by a momentous victory over Clemson that few saw coming. The Tigers swaggered into Big Thursday undefeated, ranked No. 14 nationally and as 20-point favorites over a Gamecocks squad that owned but one victory on the year to that point. "It was a foregone conclusion this morning that the contest would be dull and one-sided with the Gamecocks in for a frightful afternoon," wrote correspondent E.M. Hitt Jr. of Charleston's *Evening Post*.

It proved anything but. Before a record crowd of twenty-three thousand in the newly named Carolina Stadium, and despite star tailback Al Grygo limited by an injury, South Carolina came out with a passing attack that staggered Clemson and put the Gamecocks in complete control. Minutes into the game, Stan Stasica unleashed a 46-yard pass to Harvey Blouin that set up a 20-yard touchdown strike from Ken Roskie to Dutch Elston. Stasica found Roskie for another score to make it 12–0, and Grygo came off the bench after a Clemson turnover to rumble in for a touchdown that put the surging Gamecocks ahead, 18–0.

The Tigers looked "helpless, sluggish and somewhat amazed," Hitt wrote, as the crowd in Columbia anticipated the end of their losing streak in the rivalry. But Clemson made them sweat it out, closing to within 18–14 and leaving "the embattled Gamecocks fighting desperately in the shadows of their own goal posts until the final minute," Abe Fennell of *The State* wrote from the scene. The Tigers reached the South Carolina 17-yard line, but no farther, "as the Gamecocks fought with every ounce of strength and stamina at their command."

The result was pandemonium. South Carolina fans swarmed the field, running right through the formation of the Clemson drill platoon in the process. Church bells rang out in Columbia. "They started taking the state capital apart right then," Hitt wrote in the Charleston paper's account, "and late tonight the whooping-up was gathering momentum, foreboding one of the most exciting evenings since Sherman and his men passed this way during the Great Misunderstanding."

University president J. Rion McKissick—indeed, the former pistol-toting sophomore from the near-riot on the Horseshoe following the Clemson game

The University of South Carolina campus was transformed during World War II as many students—football players among them—joined military training programs preparing them to serve in the conflict overseas. *Courtesy of South Caroliniana Library, University of South Carolina, Columbia, S.C.*

South Carolina (*dark jerseys*) boasted a promising football team for the 1942 season, only to see many of its players, coaches and support personnel scattered across the globe during World War II. *Courtesy of South Caroliniana Library, University of South Carolina, Columbia, S.C.*

of 1902—declared the next day a school holiday. Enright, a former player under Knute Rockne at Notre Dame whose $5,000 annual salary was the highest ever paid to a South Carolina football coach, would be presented with a new Cadillac three weeks later as a reward for snapping the drought against Clemson. "Rex can start buying Columbia property now," Hitt wrote. "He can pass the rest of his days here, so far as university people are concerned."

For South Carolina, the 1941 victory represented the first ripple in what would become an unprecedented wave of success against its Upstate rival, whom the Gamecocks would defeat eight times in their next fourteen meetings. But there were more pressing issues to deal with first, and on the front page of the Columbia paper they were evident in another story just below the chronicle of the Gamecocks' thrilling victory. "Nazis claim now

South Carolina's first truly great player, Louis Sossamon, was a second-team All-American lineman for the Gamecocks in 1942 who went on to play professionally after serving in World War II. *Courtesy of University of South Carolina Athletics.*

only 35 miles from Red capital," read a much more foreboding headline, as Europe became further engulfed in war.

Just over six weeks later, with the Gamecocks having completed a 4-4-1 season that included an undefeated mark in Southern Conference play, that war would be brought to America. Sossamon, who would later be chosen as South Carolina's first All-American, joined the Navy ROTC program at the university and, like many of his teammates, waited to be summoned overseas. "Everybody seems lying quietly in wait," *Columbia Record* columnist Banjo Smith wrote, "of events that will be known only when they come to pass."

One by one they left Columbia, their departures for military service chronicled by the local paper. Back Tommy Attaway joined the navy, as did Roskie and back Buford Clary. Blouin and Steve Nowak enlisted to become U.S. Navy fliers during a recruitment event in Columbia called Naval Aviation Week. Center Bob White became a bombardier in the U.S. Army Air Corps and was stationed in England, while tackle Bobo Carter went to air corps ground school in Texas. End Gus Hempley—who had joined the army before the 1941 game against Clemson and was given a leave of absence from nearby Fort Jackson to compete for the Gamecocks—was "now across one of various ponds," Smith wrote in the *Columbia Record*.

Many other members of that 1941 team served in the U.S. Army—guard Bill Applegate, back Dewitt Arrowsmith and tackles Robert George and Joe Krivonak among them. Back Truman Hoxitt joined the U.S. Marines, where he would become an officer. Even assistant coaches were called to serve: Sterling DuPree would become an officer in the army and Ted Twomey a lieutenant in the navy's preflight program, while Charlie Treadway joined the navy. From South Carolina's sports information staff, Red Hawkins joined the marines and George Zuckerman the army. Fennell, who chronicled that 1941 Clemson-Carolina game for *The State*, would become a major in the army engineers. Even Enright would be gone by 1943, off to serve in the navy, while the Gamecocks program was overseen by three different coaches in as many seasons until his return in 1946.

Carolina Stadium earned its name in 1941 after the University of South Carolina took control of an austere former municipal facility constructed by the Works Progress Administration during the Great Depression. *Courtesy of University of South Carolina Athletics.*

And there were many others, and still more to come. Back Earl Dunham would join the army in 1943. Sossamon played the 1942 season while working as an ROTC instructor and departed in April 1943 to apply for a naval commission. He went through boot camp in Bainbridge, Maryland, served on a destroyer escort and was stationed for a time at Pearl Harbor. "We were training for the invasion of Japan," he recalled many years later. Memories of December 7, 1941, were all around him. "You could see parts of the ships that had been bombed sticking out of the water."

From a football perspective, among the biggest losses was Stasica, the All–Southern Conference halfback who had been a catalyst in the streak-busting victory over Clemson the year before and was expected to be a mainstay for the Gamecocks in the seasons to come. "Stan Stasica Will Be Drafted into Army August 1," read a banner headline in *The State* newspaper in the summer of 1942. Initially stationed at Camp Grant in Illinois, Stasica became a paratrooper and served in Europe. He was a standout on the 101st Airborne's "Skytrain" football team that would take on squads from other units, and he dabbled in minor-league football upon his return to the States.

But Stasica's career at South Carolina was over, after a spectacular sophomore season in which he had rushed for six touchdowns, passed for four scores and left the promise of so much more to come. "I would give almost anything to go back to Carolina this year, as I enjoyed my two years

34

there very much," he wrote in a letter to *The State*. "The people of South Carolina have been swell to me, and I'll miss them very much."

More players would be drafted, some even during preseason camp for the 1942 campaign, leaving Enright and his depleted staff managing a roster that could change by the day. For a while, there was doubt that the 1942 season would even be played, given the need for transportation assets for the war effort. When the opening day of practice arrived, Enright had just thirty players—one of them was Scooter Rucks, a sprinter from the South Carolina track team who had never played football before and was called upon to help bolster the Gamecocks' backfield. "Our small squad," Enright said, "will necessitate exceptional physical condition of the players."

College football programs around the country were coming to grips with a similar new reality, as the war changed the very fabric of the game. By 1942, over sixty schools had shut down their football programs due to enrollment or roster shortcomings, author Wilbur D. Jones wrote in his definitive tome of the era, *Football! Navy! War!* Rules barring freshman eligibility were waived at two-thirds of colleges. "Restrictions took over," Jones wrote. "Night games ceased on both coasts, and the government forbade special buses or trains for spectators to attend games." The rationing of gasoline and tire rubber limited travel, "resulting in game site transfers and cancellations, and a 19 percent attendance decline."

Dozens of top players, such as Northwestern's Otto Graham, Georgia's Charley Trippi and Tulsa's Glenn Dobbs, served in uniform, as did coaches like Bud Wilkinson, Jim Tatum, Don Faurot and Bear Bryant. And in the era's most notable change, the U.S. Navy and U.S. Marine Corps threw their full support behind intercollegiate football as a conditioning, teamwork and leadership exercise, leading to the creation of college football squads at military bases that would become some of the most dominant teams of their day. (The army, strangely, stuck to intramural ball, though West Point remained a national power.) Transfer rules were loosened under a program known as "lend-lease"—named after the program that shipped American war supplies to Great Britain and the Soviet Union—permitting players to switch schools even within the same season and allowing the military base teams to stock up on talent with the aim of building better officers for the war effort.

The wartime rules created juggernauts like Bainbridge Naval Training Station, led by North Carolina great Charlie "Choo Choo" Justice, which went unbeaten in 1944 and finished ranked fifth in the season's final Associated Press poll. There was also Iowa Pre-Flight, which took its name from the naval aviation training center based at the University of Iowa, was coached by Faurot and Wilkinson, and finished ranked second in the final 1943 poll. Great Lakes Navy, Del Monte Pre-Flight, March Field—navy and marine bases across the country fielded powerful squads that appeared throughout the final AP rankings during the wartime years. Their goal was winning on more than just the gridiron. "We can state confidently," Jones wrote, "that competitive, tough, conditioning football played a sizeable but little known role in helping to win the war."

And then there were programs like South Carolina, which held on to whatever it could. In the *Columbia Record*, columnist Banjo Smith railed to no avail against "Southern Conference bigwigs" who should "come down from their idealistic high horse and let freshmen play." South Carolina's roster contained members of the military reserves whose deployment status hinged on exams to come that January, as well as players who had registered for the draft but not yet been called up. The result was predictable: despite the presence of the great Sossamon, who would go on to play in the pros after his return from the Pacific, the Gamecocks would finish that wartorn 1942 campaign at 1-7-1—their worst record since 1919. A scoreless tie against Tennessee on opening day and a 14–0 victory over the Citadel in Orangeburg were the lone bright spots in an otherwise dismal season.

Rex Enright served as South Carolina's head coach from 1938 until being called to military service in 1943. After the conclusion of World War II, he would return to oversee the Gamecocks from 1946 to 1955. *Courtesy of University of South Carolina Athletics.*

"There are spots on the Gamecock team which are manned by barely enough material to get by on," Smith wrote in a portentous dispatch from South Carolina's first day of practice. "This is one football season which will be played game by game, week by week, with whatever boys happen to be left around as Uncle Sam continues his careful but steady pickings for his big party overseas."

4
LONE STAR STUNNER

He was a star halfback on the South Carolina football program, but the only running King Dixon was doing was back and forth to the bathroom. His stomach was in revolt, his temperature was climbing and his chances of playing for the Gamecocks the next day seemed remote. But when game time arrived the following evening, Dixon was in uniform and in his customary position of back to receive the opening kickoff. He cradled the football, launched forward, made a cut—and soiled his pants so badly, he later had to don a cape and duck beneath the grandstands to change.

But on that October night in 1957, no one noticed. The 38,500 spectators at Texas Memorial Stadium were instead mesmerized by the sight of Dixon running untouched for a 98-yard touchdown, the first time in twenty-four seasons that anyone had returned the opening kickoff against the Longhorns for a score. It would prove the opening volley in an incredible, back-and-forth game that produced one of the Gamecocks' biggest road victories of the era, even if the contest remains little-remembered today.

South Carolina entered that 1957 season brimming with confidence after coming off a 7-3 campaign the year before, one in which a touchdown loss to North Carolina State had kept the Gamecocks out of the Orange Bowl. They boasted one of the best backfield tandems in school history, the halfback duo of Dixon and Alex Hawkins, who had combined for 1,426 rushing yards the previous season. "This club has every opponent in the conference worried," *Sports Illustrated* claimed in its 1957 preview of the Atlantic Coast Conference.

But the Gamecocks were every bit as predictable as they were talented. After Rex Enright stepped down as football coach and athletic director following a 3-6 mark in 1955, the school hired as his successor Warren Giese, a former assistant at Maryland. Under head coach Jim Tatum, the Terrapins had won the national championship in 1953, but they did it using a grinding, run-based style. Giese would bring the same approach to Columbia, where he had the ideal personnel in Hawkins and Dixon, even if his somewhat bludgeoning strategy wasn't completely beloved.

Giese's style "was very simplistic. It was three yards and a cloud of dust. He had been on a national championship staff at Maryland, so he saw no reason to change," Hawkins told authors Rick Scoppe and Charlie Bennett years later. The Gamecocks under Giese had just one pass play, a halfback option, which meant either Hawkins was throwing to Dixon or Dixon was throwing to Hawkins. "We played really dull football," Hawkins added. "Dreadful."

South Carolina star halfbacks Alex Hawkins (*left*) and King Dixon clown for the cameras before departing Columbia for a game at national power Texas in 1957. *The State Newspaper Photograph Archive, Courtesy of Richland Library, Columbia, S.C.*

Giese had a different term for it: control football, which dominated time of possession and utilized the forward pass only sparingly. And with Hawkins on the right and Dixon on the left side of Giese's wing-T formation, the Gamecocks played control football with spectacular effectiveness. The two halfbacks were immensely skilled best friends, even if they had taken rather different paths to South Carolina and were worlds apart in terms of personality.

Dixon was the straightlaced son of a state legislator who had originally considered Duke medical school, until he witnessed a doctor cleaning gangrene out of an amputated leg and realized he didn't have the stomach for it. He would go on to spend over two decades in the marines, serve in a reconnaissance battalion in Vietnam and work as a banking executive before becoming South Carolina's athletic director during a roller-coaster period in which he oversaw both the aftermath of a steroid scandal and the school's entry into the Southeastern Conference.

Hawkins, meanwhile, was reportedly recruited to South Carolina by Enright with the promise of money and automobiles, only to see all those assurances disappear once the more discipline-minded Giese took over the program. Hawkins returned to his native West Virginia to wait for another school to call—but none did, and he wound up back in Columbia. Hawkins would go on to write two colorful memoirs about an NFL career spent mainly with the Baltimore Colts, where he was as active off the field as he was on it. "He evaded countless bed checks in training camp, sneaked out of hotels on the road, to gambol and gamble, and accrued more fines than his coaches could count," according to his obituary in the *Baltimore Sun*. Once, in San Francisco, Hawkins tied bedsheets together and lowered himself out a window—only to find coaches waiting for him. When he retired, he threw a party that lasted four days.

So, Dixon and Hawkins were an odd couple, to say the least, but on the football field, they made magic. On Dixon's 98-yard kickoff return to open the game that night in Texas in 1957, it was Hawkins who threw the key, final block at midfield that allowed his teammate to scamper to the end zone untouched. The celebration didn't last long, though; the Longhorns tied it on a 21-yard run by backup halfback Rene Ramirez, then went ahead 14–7 after quarterback Walt Fondren found Dick Schulte for an 8-yard score. After a Dixon fumble deep in Gamecocks territory, Max Alvis caught a 4-yard scoring pass that put Texas up 21–7 with eight minutes left in the third quarter.

The outcome many had expected, it seemed, was rounding into shape. Texas had entered the game as a 6-point favorite and ranked No. 20 in that week's Associated Press poll. First-year Longhorns head coach Darrell Royal had come from Washington to take over a program that had gone 1-9 under Edwin Price the season before, and improvement already appeared evident: Royal's Texas team entered the South Carolina game at 2-0, with a showdown against No. 1 Oklahoma looming the following week. Up two touchdowns in the second half against an opponent with no passing game, the Longhorns seemed on the cusp of carrying a perfect record into the Red River Showdown. With a 9:00 p.m. start time on the East Coast and much of the nation absorbed in either the World Series or the hysteria over the Soviet Sputnik satellite launched a day earlier, it had all the makings of a game that would belong only to the history books.

Head coach Warren Giese implemented a ground-oriented offense that made great use of star halfbacks Alex Hawkins and King Dixon, even if his lack of imagination wasn't always popular with players. *Courtesy of University of South Carolina Athletics.*

Even the Gamecocks had their doubts. When "you line up there and those fired-up Texans sing, 'The Eyes of Texas Are Upon You,' you know you are in a different world," Dixon told Scoppe and Bennett. "When we showed up and got off the bus, we were so small compared to the Longhorns that I think they thought we were the glee club coming out there to sing."

Giese, though, may have had a hint of what was to come. Although he had gone in with his usual game plan of "three, four, five yards at a time," with no "opening up" planned, the Gamecocks' head coach also knew that Texas would be relying heavily on sophomores—first-year players in the era before freshmen were eligible—due to a rash of injuries. The Longhorns would be especially vulnerable on the left side of their defensive line, Giese knew, so the Gamecocks pounded away at that side behind Dixon and Hawkins.

A long, grinding, typical South Carolina drive aided by a Texas personal-foul penalty resulted in a 1-yard Hawkins touchdown with 12:25 remaining, although the point-after kick was blocked. Then the Gamecocks began to get help from an unlikely source—Texas punter Bobby Lackey, who endured a miserable second half and gave South Carolina the opening it needed to

Halfback King Dixon (*20*) was a star for the Gamecocks in the late 1950s. His kickoff return marks—including his 98-yarder to open the 1957 game at Texas—long ranked at or near the top of the South Carolina record book. *The State Newspaper Photograph Archive, Courtesy of Richland Library, Columbia, S.C.*

get back in the game. One high, short Lackey punt took a backward bounce and traveled just 4 yards, which the Gamecocks converted into a 36-yard touchdown pass from Hawkins to Dixon that trimmed the margin to 1 point with eight minutes to go. South Carolina held again, and Lackey punted again—and this time, the kick went just 13 yards.

From the Texas 38, the Gamecocks set out on a drive that would become famous, capped by an 18-yard Hawkins touchdown run with 3:25 left in the game that put South Carolina ahead, 27–21. "It was a run that left the fans amazed," Ray Benson, correspondent for *The State*, wrote from the scene. "Hawkins ran through five tacklers as he set sail for the goal line. The Longhorns finally got him down as he fell across."

Hawkins, though, wasn't done. The future All-American then intercepted Fondren on the Longhorns' ensuing series, returning it to the Texas 19. A penalty for illegal receiver downfield kept the Gamecocks out of the end zone, but the possession had done its job by eating up over two minutes on the clock. Texas was left with precious little time, and the Longhorns' last-gasp drive reached only their 43-yard line before the clock ran out. Giese was carried off on the shoulders of his players, while Royal—who would go on to win 167 games and three national championships—suffered his first loss with the Longhorns, in the stadium that in 1996 would be renamed in his honor.

Across the nation, the result was shock, with the Associated Press referring to the Gamecocks as a "lightly-held South Carolina team." Within Texas, there was disbelief. "I don't see how they came back," *San Antonio News* sports editor Johnny James wrote of the Gamecocks, according to *The State*. Meanwhile, he added, "Texas' new look in football designs came apart at the seams." For South Carolina, it was the program's most notable nonconference road victory since a win at No. 18 Army in 1954.

South Carolina's jubilant flight home was on a Pan Am aircraft that had come by way of Buenos Aires and featured an international crew whose members knew little or nothing about this strange American game. When the Gamecocks stepped off the plane in Columbia, they were all wearing Stetson-style hats that had been given to them by a Texas booster club. Giese even sported silver spurs, another gift from the Lone Star State. While his team had been outgained 326–207, he knew what had turned the tide. "Texas had a lot of sophomores in the lineup and the pressure was on," Giese told reporters after disembarking. "They just didn't have the necessary experience."

The victory at Texas, which, despite its poor record the previous season, had been a national title contender for much of the early 1950s, stoked anticipation for the remainder of South Carolina's 1957 campaign. "The Gamecocks are now in excellent position to match their 7-3 record of last year," columnist Jake Penland wrote in *The State*. But the optimism didn't stop there; Penland also mused about the possibility of "an 8-2 record that would be the best in the university's history."

Others took a more cautious stance. "To the average football fan who champions the garnet and black of USC, the victory over Texas was a great gridiron upset, to be ranked alongside the one over Army a few years back," Doug Donehue wrote in the *News and Courier* of Charleston. "But to the fan who goes deeper than the final score, South Carolina's victory over Texas wasn't so surprising. Texas is in the process of rebuilding. The Longhorns have a new coach and a sophomore-studded squad which actually isn't looked upon as a 'big power' by anybody, least of all the other schools in the Southwest Conference."

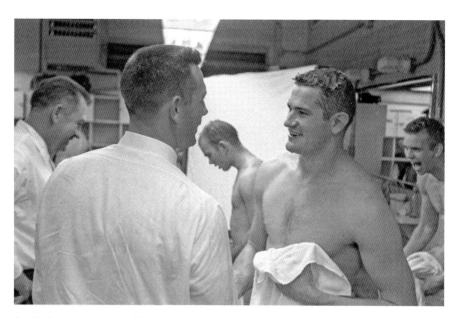

South Carolina players celebrate in the locker room after winning, 27–21, at Texas in 1957. *The State Newspaper Photograph Archive, Courtesy of Richland Library, Columbia, S.C.*

His words would prove prophetic. After the Gamecocks blitzed Furman to improve to 3-1, they were undone by a series of losses in ACC play. A late-season knee injury to Dixon didn't help, and the final result was a 5-5 record that was a bitter disappointment given how the campaign had begun. The potential shown on that night in Texas wasn't realized until the following season, 1958, when a victory over 10th-ranked Clemson sparked South Carolina to a 7-3 mark and a 15th-place position in the final Associated Press poll—the first time the Gamecocks had appeared in the year-end ranking, and their lone appearance until they finished 11th after the 1984 campaign.

But that victory at Texas—still the lone meeting between the two programs—was not soon forgotten, especially after the Longhorns rebounded from the loss to finish 6-4-1 and make the Sugar Bowl. Years later, when checking into a hotel in San Antonio, Dixon was asked by the front desk clerk if it was his first visit to the Lone Star State. The old Gamecock halfback couldn't help himself.

"Ma'am, I visited back here in [1957] and I ran the opening kickoff back against the University of Texas for 98 yards when coach Darrell Royal was here in his first year," Dixon replied. Later, he mused, "I don't know what prompted me to say that. But it just felt good to say it out there, and to be back out there."

5
BLACK FRIDAY

Marvin Bass sat in a rocking chair outside his room at the Heart of Columbia Motel, having just completed bed check for his South Carolina football team. It was the usual routine for the Gamecocks, who were bunkered down in the lodgings they used on the night before every home game and were anticipating the annual rivalry showdown with Clemson set for the next day. But there was hardly anything usual about this Friday. And when Bass saw sports information director Tom Price approaching in the darkness, South Carolina's head coach knew it wouldn't be a normal Saturday, either.

Price was there to deliver news that Bass was expecting: there would be no game the following day. It was after ten o'clock in the evening, hours after shots had rung out in downtown Dallas, and President John F. Kennedy had slumped over in his open-topped limousine. But in Columbia and elsewhere, the shock had yet to subside. City after city reported an eerie stillness as Americans struggled to absorb the fact that a young, dynamic president had been murdered in broad daylight in the heart of a major city. How could anyone play a football game the next day?

In Columbia, the final decision on whether the Gamecocks and Tigers would play came only after hours of handwringing and indecisiveness. For sports leagues and individual programs in the fall of 1963, there was no handbook on how to proceed in the aftermath of a presidential assassination—something the nation hadn't endured since William McKinley was gunned down sixty-two years earlier. In the age before the internet, social media and twenty-four-hour all-sports cable networks, it was difficult for colleges like South Carolina to gauge who was doing what and to follow the consensus. In the wake of Kennedy's death, programs were having to make decisions on their own while mostly in the dark about how others were proceeding and unsure of what the public reaction would be.

Red Smith of the *New York Herald-Tribune*, the most influential sports columnist in America, argued that the nation needed "a day of mourning." Football programs, South Carolina and Clemson among them, groped blindly for the right thing to do. Perhaps that's why, initially, South Carolina president Thomas F. Jones and Clemson president Robert C. Edwards had agreed that the game would go on as scheduled—only to reverse themselves that evening after conferring again.

Earlier in the week, concerns in the Palmetto State had been far more conventional. The Gamecocks were on the verge of their worst football campaign since World War I, buried underneath a 1-7-1 record and coming off a brutal loss at Wake Forest in which the Demon Deacons had snapped a nineteen-game losing streak. Bass was under constant scrutiny, and South Carolina was bracing for a Clemson squad that sported only a .500 record

South Carolina head coach Marvin Bass *(far left)* meets with CBS producers during the week of the Clemson game in 1963. The contest was to be broadcast regionally by the network, a plan scrapped after the assassination of President John F. Kennedy. *The State Newspaper Photograph Archive, Courtesy of Richland Library, Columbia, S.C.*

but had won four straight games and in many eyes was playing the best football in the ACC.

These were lean, trying times for the Gamecocks, and the student body could sense it. So, for practice on the Thursday evening before the Clemson game—the Big Thursday tradition had been ended in 1959—roughly three thousand South Carolina students showed up, ringing the practice field and voicing their support. Chanting slogans such as "We like Bass, we like Bass," the students provided a dose of moral support to players and staff members who sorely needed it and propelled the Gamecocks to their most spirited practice session of the week.

"This will help us Saturday," Gamecocks quarterback Dan Reeves told the local paper afterward. "I only wish we had this kind of support earlier in the year. It's good to see people still believe in us. We'll want to win this one Saturday for all these people." Bass was equally as moved. "It was the most enthusiastic showing I've seen at the university. And it might provide the spark we need," the head coach said.

Less than twenty-four hours later, such concerns would seem almost trivial. *The State* newspaper ran a large photo of Gamecocks players, still wearing their practice gear, gathered around a television to watch news coverage of the Kennedy assassination. Farther west, Clemson was in the dark about what had happened—the Tigers had departed campus by bus at noon Eastern time, about ninety minutes before Lee Harvey Oswald fired his fatal shots from the sixth floor of the Texas School Book Depository in Dallas. They were bound for Batesburg, where they traditionally stayed the night before games in Columbia. Passing through Saluda, line coach Bob Smith noticed that the flag in front of the post office was at half-staff.

But he didn't know the reason why until they reached their hotel at 3:00 p.m., about an hour after Kennedy had been pronounced dead at Parkland Memorial Hospital. Unsure of the game's status for the next day, the Tigers went ahead with a scheduled practice at a local high school. Clemson head coach Frank Howard could see his players' hearts just weren't in it.

"We were up, but after our boys heard of the President's death, things started to happen," Howard told *The State* columnist Jake Penland. "There were busted signals, with two boys running together—things like that. They didn't have their minds on football."

It was a similar situation at South Carolina, where Bass saw "a marked change in our players at practice after they heard news of the President's death," he said, according to Penland. "They were lining up in the wrong formations, and so on. Their minds were not on football."

Gamecocks head coach Marvin Bass at a pep rally prior to the 1963 game against Clemson. South Carolina entered the contest at 1-7-1, with one last chance to try and salvage the season. *The State Newspaper Photograph Archive, Courtesy of Richland Library, Columbia, S.C.*

At that point, though, every indication was that they would be asked to play the following day. Across the country, the assassination had prompted waves of postponements and cancellations—including major horseracing events, championship boxing matches and some NBA games. But no sport faced a more vexing decision than football, which had been the president's favorite. He had been an undersized halfback at Harvard, where each of his three brothers had also played, and the Kennedy touch football games on the lawn of the family estate in Hyannis Port, Massachusetts, had become a beloved scene of Americana. When NFL commissioner Pete Rozelle reached out to Kennedy press secretary Pierre Salinger about whether to play that following Sunday, he was reminded that football had been the president's game.

The NFL went forward, a move Rozelle would later regret to his dying day. There were no pregame festivities, no player introductions and no television coverage—all cameras were still focused on events in Dallas, where Oswald would also meet his demise at an assassin's bullet. Players were moved to tears as "Taps" was played by a bugler. Columnists across the country derided Rozelle as heartless, and the universal negative reaction to the NFL playing in the wake of the Kennedy assassination almost surely played into the league's decision to postpone games in the aftermath of the terrorist attacks on New York and Washington on September 11, 2001, a move almost every other pro and college league followed.

But in 1963, the NFL was not yet the American sports trendsetter it would become, and there was no national guidance for schools like South Carolina to follow. One college game was even played on the day of the assassination itself—Wake Forest was in Raleigh, North Carolina, eating lunch before a game that Friday afternoon against North Carolina State when news that Kennedy had been shot interrupted regular television programming. Since the Deacons had already arrived, NC State chancellor John T. Caldwell and Wake Forest president Harold Tribble decided their schools would play. "I learned that our players desired to play the game as scheduled," Caldwell said later of the Wolfpack's 42–0 victory, adding, "I deeply believe that President Kennedy would have wished the game to go on."

With the college football schedule in its final regular-season weekend and a number of games on tap that would determine major bowl bids, the NCAA let colleges make the decision for themselves. Executive director Walter Byers stipulated only that any games played include "an appropriate, dignified opening ceremony and whatever other memorial tribute you might think appropriate at half-time." At South Carolina, Price returned to the stadium after learning of the assassination to find the CBS crew packing up its gear. South Carolina and Clemson were to receive $53,000 each for regional CBS television coverage of the game, but around-the-clock news broadcasts left no airtime for sports.

Meanwhile, Bass, Howard and their respective players continued their numb preparations, always with one eye on the television. Price made the media rounds in Columbia, notifying reporters that the game was still on the next day, then repaired to Swain's Steak House for dinner with Bob Bradley, his counterpart at Clemson. Suddenly, he was summoned to the telephone. Jones, the university president, was on the line informing him that the decision made earlier in the day had been changed, and the game had been rescheduled for 2:00 p.m. on Thanksgiving Day.

Why did the two university presidents reverse course? In its news story the following morning, *The State* did not offer an explanation. At 10:00 p.m., the schools issued a joint statement: "The Clemson vs. South Carolina football game scheduled for November 23, 1963 has been postponed due to the death of President John F. Kennedy," it read. "We regret any inconvenience

President John F. Kennedy, here attending an Army-Navy game, was a great fan of football. It was difficult for many leagues and universities to decide whether to play in the days following his assassination in 1963. *Courtesy John F. Kennedy Presidential Library and Museum.*

that may be caused to individual fans, but we feel this action is in accord with the solemnity of the hour."

Price was asked to inform the Gamecocks football team, and Bass was relieved at the news. "Postponement of the game was the right thing to do, without question," the Gamecocks' coach told Penland. "It would have been pretty tough in the stadium today for everybody. How could they stand during a prayer for the late President? And get in the spirit of a football game? I would have felt guilty."

Over in Batesburg, Clemson decided to immediately return to campus, and by 10:30 p.m. they were back on the road. Postponing the game "was the only thing to do," Howard said. "I don't think either team would have played well if the game had gone on as scheduled today."

Although it took a late-night reconsideration by the two university presidents, history would indicate that the Gamecocks and Tigers

Left: University of South Carolina president Thomas F. Jones initially decided, along with Clemson president Robert C. Edwards, that the Gamecocks and Tigers would play as scheduled on the day after President Kennedy's assassination. Hours later, they changed their minds. *Courtesy of South Caroliniana Library, University of South Carolina, Columbia, S.C.*

Below: South Carolina players take the field for a 1963 game against Clemson that was postponed five days until Thanksgiving following the assassination of President Kennedy. *The State Newspaper Photograph Archive, Courtesy of Richland Library, Columbia, S.C.*

ultimately made the right decision. According to the online college football database at Sports Reference, there were only seventeen college football games played the day after the Kennedy assassination, as opposed to sixty-one games played the previous Saturday. Some games that went on were notable, such as Nebraska versus Oklahoma for a bid to the Orange Bowl, a game involving Texas Christian—a school in Fort Worth, where Kennedy had spent the night before he was shot—and the entire SEC slate. But the schools that cancelled or postponed their matchups for that bleak weekend never had to issue explanations or face second-guessing about why they took to the field that day.

But even five days later, the pall remained. The flag outside South Carolina's stadium flew at half-mast, and the Clemson band played a tribute to Kennedy. A spectator from Easley died of an apparent heart attack, and there were a few skirmishes in the grandstands. Many officials, including Governor Donald Russell and other top state officeholders, skipped the game because they had already made Thanksgiving plans. The crowd was about six thousand shy of capacity, and tickets that would regularly go for $5.75 were being sold outside the stadium for $0.50.

It was "the saddest Big Thursday," *The State* called it, in a reference to the day of the week on which the two rivals had long previously played. And South Carolina let a halftime lead slip away, succumbing to Clemson's "bone-crushing ground attack" to fall, 24–20. Twice the desperate Gamecocks went for it on fourth-and-short in their own territory. Both times they were halted, and both times Clemson converted the stops into scores, part of a run of 17 straight points that saddled South Carolina with its worst record since 1919.

In the locker room afterward, tears welled up in Bass's eyes as he addressed his team. It had been a hard season, and a harder week, in Columbia and beyond. "I hate to wish my life away," he later told reporters. "But this is one year I'll be glad is over."

6

CARDIAC CHAMPIONS

Sleet fell and temperatures hovered around freezing on a cold Saturday in Winston-Salem, North Carolina, but inside the visitor's locker room at Groves Stadium, the atmosphere was joyous and warm. South Carolina football players sang, smiled and shouted, dressing in the afterglow of a championship three-quarters of a century in the making. On the flight home, head coach Paul Dietzel couldn't help himself. "This is your pilot," he announced to all aboard the chartered jet. "We are now approaching Columbia, home of the ACC champions."

Upon touchdown at Columbia's airport, more revelry awaited. Several hundred fans huddled in the cold on that November evening in 1969, ready to welcome home the team that, after seventy-four years of football, had at last secured the program's first championship of any kind. People brought signs and horns and their small children to witness a homecoming like no South Carolina fans had ever seen before. Dietzel shook hands and signed autographs. There was one more regular-season game remaining, against rival Clemson, but only pride would be on the line. The events of that brisk Saturday had clinched South Carolina's first Atlantic Coast Conference crown.

"We're finally on the map, Coach," one well-wisher shouted to Dietzel.

The title had been secured that day after South Carolina went to Winston-Salem and used three touchdown passes from standout quarterback Tommy Suggs to dispatch Wake Forest, 24–6. For the Gamecocks to earn the crown outright, they also needed Clemson to lose at North Carolina. With five minutes remaining on the clock at Groves Stadium and the game in hand, Dietzel asked South Carolina's team doctor for the Clemson score. Told that North Carolina had won, 32–15, the Gamecocks' head coach allowed himself a smile. The celebration was on.

But the championship itself—South Carolina's first outright title not just in football, but in any varsity sport—had been months in the making. Dietzel, who had won a national championship at LSU in 1958, had been hired four years earlier to reverse the direction of a program that had struggled under his predecessor, Marvin Bass. Two of his first three campaigns at South Carolina had resulted in losing records, but the 1968 season had closed with a narrow victory over Clemson that portended better things. Dietzel knew he had a strong roster coming back, and for one of the few times in Gamecocks football history, a conference title seemed like a realistic prospect—even though South Carolina hadn't enjoyed so much as a winning season in a decade.

"The Gamecocks, for one of the rare times in their sordid football history, seem to have a chance at winning a championship," executive sports editor Herman Helms wrote in *The State* in September 1969. He added: "Nothing

South Carolina head coach Paul Dietzel (*left*) confers with quarterback Tommy Suggs on the sideline during a game in the Gamecocks' 1969 ACC championship season. *The State Newspaper Photograph Archive, Courtesy of Richland Library, Columbia, S.C.*

is impossible. The Mets are leading the league, and the Jets did beat the Colts, and men did walk on the moon."

Even Dietzel seemed optimistic. "We should have the best defensive team we've had during my years at USC," he said in the preseason. "We should also have the most varied [offensive] attack that we've had. We should have the best overall squad we've had."

There was certainly talent on the roster to inspire hope. Suggs was a proven quarterback and a gritty leader who had who passed for 1,544 yards and thirteen touchdowns the season before. Fullback Warren Muir, who had scored five touchdowns in the 1968 season, was in Dietzel's view "the best inside runner in college football." Linebacker Al Usher was among the best at his position in the ACC. And receiver Fred Ziegler was an All-ACC performer despite hardly looking the part—at five feet, ten inches tall and 183 pounds, sporting thick glasses off the field, the former walk-on was "slow and couldn't block a lick," his head coach once said. But he possessed a knack for running routes and making cuts at top speed and was fearless when it came to catching passes in traffic.

Suggs recalls strong recruiting classes that bolstered the Gamecocks' roster and summer workouts that heightened camaraderie on a team loaded with savvy, veteran players. "We felt confident, but you never know," the former quarterback said. "But we felt like we could play with anybody going into the season."

There were concerns, like a secondary in which Dietzel would have to start two sophomores—one of them being Bo Davies, who would go on to set the school's career record for interceptions. There was a flu bug that swept through the locker room the week before the season opener, forcing a number of players to miss practice. And then there was a frontloaded schedule in which the Gamecocks would face what appeared to be their two main challengers for the ACC title, Duke and North Carolina State, within the season's first month. If South Carolina was indeed a legitimate championship contender, it would find out right away.

So, anticipation was high for a season opener at Carolina Stadium against a Duke program the Gamecocks had beaten just once in the previous ten years. The game was a sellout, and the highway patrol urged fans to leave home at least two hours early if they hoped to be in their seats by kickoff. The 43,000 spectators in attendance would witness one of the more thrilling games in South Carolina history, one that Duke led, 17–13, after Blue Devils quarterback Leo Hart found Wes Chesson in the end zone from 18 yards out with 11:57 to play.

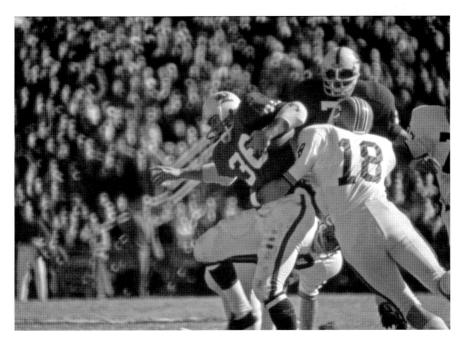

Called "the best inside runner in college football" by coach Paul Dietzel, Warren Muir (*36*) was a powerful fullback for the Gamecocks who helped provide South Carolina with a well-rounded offense during its ACC championship season of 1969. *The State Newspaper Photograph Archive, Courtesy of Richland Library, Columbia, S.C.*

From there, it swung back and forth. Facing a fourth-and-2 on South Carolina's ensuing possession, Suggs ran a read-option play in which he faked a handoff to Muir and watched the Duke defense collapse on the star running back. The quarterback darted through a hole at right tackle and ran untouched to the end zone for a 48-yard touchdown that put the Gamecocks back on top, 20–17. "I knew I had the first down, but once we got outside, [the Duke defenders] were all on Warren," Suggs said later. "No one was there. I turned upfield, got a great block and no one got within five, 10 yards of me."

Afterward, Dietzel would refer to that fourth-down call as "the biggest gamble of my coaching career." But for the Gamecocks, there was more gambling to come. Duke counterpunched, tying the game, 20–20, on a 43-yard field goal with 6:20 remaining. Starting from his own 25, Suggs then engineered a drive that included a 16-yard pass to Dick Harris and a 24-yard connection to Ziegler—the latter on another gamble, a fourth-and-1 from the Duke 37. Down at the Duke 4, Dietzel eschewed the field-goal attempt,

Effective with his feet as well as his arm, South Carolina quarterback Tommy Suggs dashed for a 48-yard rushing touchdown that proved crucial in a victory over Duke to open the Gamecocks' 1969 season. *The State Newspaper Photograph Archive, Courtesy of Richland Library, Columbia, S.C.*

and the Gamecocks went for it yet again on fourth down, this time with Rudy Holloman converting by barreling down to the 2. One play later, Muir crashed into the end zone behind left tackle for a score with 1:25 left that cemented a 27–20 victory in a critical ACC opener.

"It was a must-have drive," Suggs said years later, "one you've got to have if you're going to win the ACC."

The fourth-down calls never intimidated Dietzel—much like another South Carolina coach, Steve Spurrier, would do many years later, he knew the odds and how they played to his team's favor more than the nervous fans in the grandstands might have thought. Dietzel also possessed a quiet courage that had been forged decades earlier, when he piloted a B-29 Superfortress in fire-bombing raids over Japan during World War II. The raids were flown below ten thousand feet, so low that crews could feel the heat from the fires erupting below. "You wondered if you were going to make it out of there," said Dietzel, who died in 2013 at age eighty-nine.

"He had an inner strength and toughness that sometimes didn't come through" to those watching from afar, Suggs remembered. "He'd also take a chance."

In Columbia, the season-opening victory over Duke brought elation mixed with relief. The Gamecocks had made crucial plays to win a close game against a foe considered to be one of the best in the league, a stark contrast to their fortunes in recent years. Little did Gamecocks supporters know that two more roller-coaster games still stood between South Carolina and its first ACC championship—including another coming the next week.

Unlike Duke, North Carolina wasn't expected to be a contender for the ACC crown in 1969. The Tar Heels started eleven first-year players, including quarterback Johnny Swofford, who would later become the league's commissioner (and be better known as John). The season before, South Carolina had rallied from 27–3 down in the fourth quarter to stun the Tar Heels in Chapel Hill—North Carolina head coach Bill Dooley had called it "the most crushing blow I've had to take in football"—so UNC seemed little more than a speed bump before the much more difficult games to come.

It turned into anything but. "Another Gamecock Thrill Show," a headline in *The State* called it, after the young Tar Heels had pushed South Carolina to the brink. There was another deficit—this time 6–0 at halftime—that necessitated another comeback, this one after a miserable opening two quarters of football in which little had gone right for the home team. Defense had kept South Carolina in the game, holding North Carolina to just a pair of Don Hartig field goals, while the Gamecocks' vaunted offensive attack had been mistake-prone and ineffective, managing just one first down—until a third quarter that *The State* executive sports editor Herman Helms called "a display of near-perfect football."

It started with, who else, Suggs, who engineered a 54-yard drive that included a 15-yard pass to Doug Hamrick and a connection with Ziegler for 20, and ended with Muir hammering into the end zone from 6 yards out on third down. The Gamecocks held North Carolina without a first down for the length of the quarter, and a Davies interception of a Swofford pass put South Carolina in business again at the Tar Heels' 34. On third down from the 26-yard line, Suggs threw for Ziegler in the end zone, only to have the ball deflected by North Carolina cornerback Rusty Culbreth. But the acrobatic Ziegler still snared it, and suddenly the Gamecocks led 14–6 with 1:05 left in the quarter.

"That was a spectacular catch," Dietzel would say after the game. North Carolina put one last scare into the Carolina Stadium crowd, but a final drive ended at the Gamecocks' 7-yard line after Dick Harris intercepted Tar Heel backup quarterback Paul Miller with twenty-two

Once viewed as too slow to play at South Carolina, receiver Fred Ziegler (*80*) evolved into an All-ACC player who made one acrobatic catch after another for the Gamecocks during their championship season of 1969. *The State Newspaper Photograph Archive, Courtesy of Richland Library, Columbia, S.C.*

seconds remaining. South Carolina had been outgained by over 100 yards, but once again the Gamecocks had found a way. Now they were 2-0 in the ACC and very much in the thick of the race for the program's first conference championship.

A blowout loss the next week at nationally ranked and nonconference Georgia did nothing to change that. South Carolina's focus quickly shifted to the following week and its next ACC game, against the opponent that on paper seemed its toughest competition for the league title: North Carolina State. Under head coach Earle Edwards, the Wolfpack had won or shared four ACC titles in the previous six seasons, and it presented a bruising ground game led by halfback Charlie Bowers. NC State had stumbled on opening weekend and suffered a stunning loss to Wake Forest, but nobody in Columbia was taking the Wolfpack lightly. To win the ACC, this was the game that South Carolina needed to have.

And it would be another nail-biter in Carolina Stadium, with the Gamecocks forced to overcome another deficit. At halftime, South Carolina trailed, 3–0, after missing a pair of field-goal attempts and having a drive stopped on fourth down at the Wolfpack 3-yard line. With 7:05 left in the third quarter, North Carolina State pushed its advantage to 10–0 after halfback Leon Mason rumbled in from 2 yards out to cap a 73-yard drive.

But when Harris—who had picked off North Carolina's last-gasp pass attempt in the final seconds the week before—caught the ensuing kickoff, everything changed. The sophomore returned it 45 yards to give both the crowd and the home team a needed spark, and Suggs took advantage by engineering an eight-play drive that got the Gamecocks back into the game. The quarterback found Rudy Holloman for completions of 22 and 17 yards, and South Carolina got down to the Wolfpack 1-yard line before facing fourth down. The gambler Dietzel rolled the dice again, and Billy Ray Rice dove off left tackle to get the Gamecocks on the board with 3:35 remaining in the third quarter.

They weren't finished yet. The South Carolina defense held, forcing North Carolina State to punt. Assistant coach Bill Rowe had recommended setting up an inside return for sophomore Jimmy Mitchell, believing the Wolfpack kick coverage to be vulnerable in that area. Mitchell took advantage, returning the punt 72 yards for a touchdown that put the Gamecocks ahead, 14–10, with 1:35 left in the third quarter. "Our biggest touchdown of the year," Dietzel called it. Muir added a fourth-quarter touchdown that capped a 69-yard drive, the Gamecocks' Pat Watson intercepted the two-point conversion try after a late Wolfpack touchdown and South Carolina recovered an onside kick attempt that snuffed out NC State's final breath.

For the Gamecocks, it was a monumental victory over the league's power team of the era, not to mention a gut check for a program that had rallied to win a close conference game for the third time in as many outings. "I'll remember Saturday night for a long time," Dietzel said afterward. No one knew at the time that NC State would turn out to be a terrible disappointment, finishing at 3-6-1 overall. All that mattered was that the Gamecocks had emerged from the toughest part of their conference schedule undefeated, even though it had taken one dramatic turn after another to get them there. South Carolina was now clearly the team to beat for the ACC championship, a fact that would have seemed unbelievable just three years earlier.

"It was beginning to feel special," Suggs recalled. "Some players were stepping up as we anticipated they would, and we had a few nice surprises. We also came together culturally as a team and a program, given that [for juniors] it was our third year. And we should have been getting it—the program was getting to be established, and we were hitting our rhythm."

After winning a nonconference squeaker over Virginia Tech, the Gamecocks easily dispatched Maryland, 17–0, behind touchdowns from

Muir and Holloman, placing themselves on the cusp of the title. Three weeks later, in their next ACC game on that cold day at Wake Forest, they had it. South Carolina capped the regular season with a 27–13 victory over Clemson in which they ran out to a 17–0 lead, generated 517 yards of total offense and sewed up a perfect record in league play. The Gamecocks hadn't just won the title—they had dominated the league, finishing three games in the win column better than anyone else.

Returning to Columbia after clinching the title at Wake Forest and seeing the crowd at the airport to welcome their champion Gamecocks home is a memory that remains vivid to Suggs today. "I'll never forget it, getting off the plane and seeing how exited everybody was," he said. "You go to a university to play sports to experience something like that, and be a part of it. And to see that many people excited, it was very special. My mother and daddy kept scrapbooks all throughout my high school and college years, and periodically I'll go into my office at home in Columbia and flip through them, seeing the pictures and reading the articles. They're great memories, and you can never take them away."

The Gamecocks' reward was a berth in the Peach Bowl, played then at Georgia Tech's Grant Field, against a West Virginia squad that had gone 10-1 as an independent and featured as head coach Jim Carlen—who in 1975 would take over the reins of the South Carolina program. The game became a quagmire, played in a heavy rain that turned the field into a sea of mud, and the conditions played right into the hands of a Mountaineers team that featured a power running game. The Gamecocks managed just five first downs and 190 total yards and scored their only points when a 37-yard field-goal attempt by kicker Billy DuPree hit the crossbar and bounced over.

"Our offense never had a chance," Gamecocks assistant coach Larry Jones said afterward. West Virginia rushed for 356 yards and won, 14–3, in a game that wasn't that close.

"It's unusual to walk on a field before the game and get in mud up to your ankles," Dietzel said. Still, he didn't blame the conditions. "Everyone could tell what the field was like. You saw it. The Gamecocks don't need excuses. We were both playing on the same field, and it wasn't any worse for them than for us."

It was a disappointing ending to South Carolina's greatest season to that point and the campaign that produced what remains the lone conference championship for the Gamecocks' football program. It proved a tough act to follow—mainstays like Muir and Ziegler graduated, South Carolina was besieged by injuries and not even the presence of the

Head coach Paul Dietzel and the Gamecocks returned to Columbia to a cheering crowd after clinching South Carolina's first championship in football with a victory at Wake Forest in 1969. *The State Newspaper Photograph Archive, Courtesy of Richland Library, Columbia, S.C.*

steady senior Suggs behind center could prevent the Gamecocks from tumbling to a 4-6-1 mark in 1970. The year after that, the Gamecocks would leave the ACC, a move championed by both Dietzel and South Carolina basketball coach Frank McGuire. There wouldn't be another conference championship to play for in football until 1992, when South Carolina entered the Southeastern Conference.

The decision by South Carolina—a charter member of the ACC—to leave the conference and become an independent would be the subject of debate for years to come. From a Gamecocks perspective, there were inequalities in the application of admission standards, and games against league rivals became physical bordering on violent as animosity bubbled over. On March 29, 1971, board of trustees chairman T. Eston Marchant announced the university's plans to leave the ACC that August. At the time, both the university and the league hoped the split would be brief. "We hope that this separation will be of a temporary nature and for a minimum amount of time," the university's statement read. It turned out to be permanent.

"[Dietzel] and coach McGuire wanted us out of the ACC, and at that time I think it was the right decision," recalled Suggs, who became a successful insurance executive and analyst on Gamecock football radio broadcasts.

"It was getting dangerous in that conference, and coach Dietzel along with coach McGuire felt things were not being equal. [Dietzel] also wanted to take the program to another level in football, and in the ACC at that time, he felt it would be hard to do that. He wanted to be on the plane with Alabama and Georgia and Tennessee at that time. He was ahead of his time, and it was controversial. But in the long run, it worked out."

But that ACC championship would leave an enduring impact, even after the Gamecocks left the conference. After practice one day prior to the Clemson game, Dietzel called his players into a conference room and revealed a model of an expanded and updated Carolina Stadium, complete with new seating decks and other improvements that would soon be in the works. Sellouts had become the norm, season ticket sales had ballooned and the stadium would need to accommodate all the additional interest in Gamecocks football that the 1969 season had generated. South Carolina was beginning to take its first steps into the era that would follow, and the program's first title was the catalyst to it all.

"That 1969 team," tackle Dave DeCamilla said years later, "put [South Carolina] on the path to the next level."

7

The Birth of Williams-Brice

The cardboard model of an expanded Carolina Stadium that Gamecocks head coach Paul Dietzel showed his players before the Clemson game in 1969 would soon become his constant traveling companion. Also serving as South Carolina's athletic director, Dietzel would ultimately assume another role—evangelist for his vision of what the home of the Gamecocks' football program needed to become.

The model "got all beat up" Dietzel remembered, as he dragged it from one gathering to another trying to raise the funds necessary to pull the university's football stadium into a more modern era. He had good reason to demand change, given that Carolina Stadium's capacity of forty-three thousand was roughly the same as it had been three decades earlier, and the success of the 1969 ACC championship team had produced regular sellouts. "If you stood up, you'd better sit down quickly, or your seat was gone," Dietzel recalled.

There was also pressure from other schools in the region, which were forging ahead with expanded stadiums that could hold more spectators and generate more revenue. In 1965, Legion Field in Birmingham, the primary home of Alabama football, had been expanded to 68,821. Georgia had expanded Sanford Stadium to 59,200 in 1967, and one year later, Tennessee expanded Neyland Stadium to 64,429. Clemson was regularly adding seats to Memorial Stadium, which by 1978 would accommodate over 53,000 spectators. The facility wars in college football were still years away, but South Carolina was already feeling the need to keep up.

Then there were the aesthetics of Carolina Stadium, a facility with a stark exterior stemming from its birth as a municipal stadium constructed in the midst of the Great Depression and built in part by the federal Works Progress Administration. The city of Columbia raised $82,000 through the sale of municipal bonds to fund the stadium, which originally held 17,600 spectators, but the money wasn't enough. As a cost-cutting move, designers chose to eliminate architectural features—the reason why South Carolina's stadium lacks the grand old archways or intricate stonework found at so many other major college facilities built in the early 1900s. Carolina Stadium remained surrounded by a wooden fence built in the 1930s and overall was "not very attractive," Dietzel recalled in a much later interview.

For a football program that appeared on the brink of taking a great leap forward, stadium improvements and expansion were quickly becoming a necessity. University leadership agreed, and by 1970—no doubt spurred by the sellout crowds of the ACC championship campaign of the previous season—work was underway on the first of what would ultimately become a four-phase expansion project that would cost $70 million in total and increase the capacity of Carolina Stadium to seventy thousand. The funding plan called for the project to be financed by a $1 seat tax, a special student activities fee and a contribution of a meager $100,000 (equal to $681,000 in 2019) from the South Carolina athletic department. Clearly, the university would need to find other ways to help cover the cost of one of the most ambitious building projects in its history.

An unexpected windfall would arrive courtesy of a woman who most Gamecocks fans had never heard of until that point. Her name was Martha Williams Brice, and she was the daughter of O.L. Williams, a Sumter businessman whose family enterprise, Williams Furniture Company, grew into one of the world's largest manufacturers of bedroom furniture before it was bought by Georgia-Pacific in 1968. Martha Brice was familiar with Gamecocks lore, given that her husband, Tom Brice, had played football for South Carolina, later graduated from the university's law school and "took great interest in the entre athletic program throughout his life," according to two nephews. Martha Brice died on September 2, 1969, and her will stipulated that a "large sum" of money be given to the university, with the amount determined by her heirs—nephews Phillip and Thomas Edwards.

The exact amount of the gift, initially unknown, captivated Columbia, and local reporters worked diligently to unearth details. In late 1970,

Above: By the 1950s, Carolina Stadium had changed little from the spare, unadorned municipal facility that had been built during the Great Depression. *Russell Maxey Photograph Collection, Courtesy of Richland Library, Columbia, S.C.*

Left: Martha Williams Brice, whose father built a Sumter company that grew into one of the world's largest suppliers of bedroom furniture, left the University of South Carolina $3.5 million in her will. Most of it would go to upgrading the football stadium. *Courtesy of South Caroliniana Library, University of South Carolina, Columbia, S.C.*

reports began to surface that Brice's donation to the university would be in the range of $5 million—with the bulk of it earmarked for renovations to the football stadium, a fact that came as a surprise to many. The amount of the gift would eventually be confirmed as $3.5 million, which university president Thomas F. Jones called "the largest private contribution ever to an institution of higher education in the state of South Carolina." The Brice donation was a massive amount for the time, the equivalent to a donation of $23 million in 2019 dollars, accounting for inflation.

Yet the idea that most of it would go to football stadium renovations was polarizing, in more ways than one. Some saw it as a frivolous use of funds, with one anonymous member of the USC board of trustees calling it "stupidity" in an interview with a reporter from United Press International. Ultimately, the gift would be split three ways: $2.75 million would go to the athletic department for stadium improvements, $500,000 would go to the university's nursing school and $250,000 would go toward the construction of a new fine arts building on the campus of USC Coastal in Conway, which is now a separate institution known as Coastal Carolina University.

Brice—who left behind a total estate of nearly $14 million—never stipulated how exactly she wanted the gift to the university split up, leaving that decision up to her heirs. Her husband, Tom Brice, had died just a few months earlier, on June 27, his birthday. The executors of Martha Brice's will, her nephews Phillip and Thomas Edwards, said at the time that the distribution of the gift "fully carries the wishes of our aunt, Mrs. Brice." Brice did, after all, have a clear connection to the football program through her husband, who had lettered for the Gamecocks in the 1922 and 1923 seasons and earned a bit of notoriety his senior year by fumbling in the Clemson game to set up the Tigers' winning score in a 7–6 loss. "They both loved Carolina a lot," Columbia lawyer Tom Brice Hall, grandson of Thomas and Martha Brice, told *The State* newspaper in 2009 on the stadium's seventy-fifth anniversary.

The gift was more than welcomed by a South Carolina program that badly needed the funds for its ambitious stadium expansion plans. Dietzel, who for so long had beat the drum for wholesale improvements to Carolina Stadium, called the donation "momentous." He added, "It is difficult to put into words how grateful all of us at the university are to the heirs for this gift, which will be so beneficial to the continued improvement of our athletic facilities and athletic program."

The moment had to be especially gratifying to a football coach who had long been lobbying for improvements to South Carolina's aging stadium.

More than just a head football coach, Paul Dietzel also played major roles in upgrading athletic facilities, pulling South Carolina out of the ACC and improving the Gamecocks' athletic department overall. *Courtesy of University of South Carolina Athletics.*

Although Dietzel also held the title of athletic director, he routinely thought beyond the scope of his dual posts, implementing forward-thinking plans all across the Gamecocks' athletic department. Not only did he relentlessly champion the movement toward a larger and more updated stadium, he also came up with the idea for the athletic dorm known as The Roost. He's credited with writing South Carolina's fight song, which was set to the tune of "Step to the Rear," a number from the Broadway musical "How Now Dow Jones." Not all of his big ideas were home runs—the installation of artificial turf at Williams-Brice Stadium made early-season games in blistering Columbia feel even hotter—but facilities and sports across the board benefited from a needed modernization under his watch.

"He was a big-picture thinker, no question about that," recalled Tommy Suggs, his quarterback on the 1969 ACC championship team. "He was an AD and a head football coach, which was somewhat common in those days. And he was an artist, and he would draw. When he retired, that's what he did—he painted. He was a renaissance guy. He was different. He was really,

South Carolina head coach Paul Dietzel gives a tour of the Gamecocks' expansive new locker rooms, built as part of the expansion and renovation of Williams-Brice Stadium in 1972. *The State Newspaper Photograph Archive, Courtesy of Richland Library, Columbia, S.C.*

really different. I don't think in many circles he gets the respect he deserves, because he was so many different things in one person. He was a really neat guy, and he clearly had a vision like nobody else."

The Brice donation would come with one notable caveat, which would be revealed in January 1971, when attorneys for the Brice estate sent a letter to Jones and board of trustees chairman T. Eston Marchant stipulating that the facilities benefiting from the gift would all carry the name "Williams-Brice." That included the football stadium, which had been called Carolina Stadium since 1941, after the city had deeded the property to the university in return for the state paying off the remaining debt. The idea of a name change didn't sit well with every member of the Gamecock fan base, as expressed in letters to the editor of the local newspaper. John W. Baxley called it "disheartening news," adding that "it is difficult to understand how $2.75 million can be such an overwhelming factor in the renaming of a stadium already owned by Carolinians."

R.B. Dunovant Jr. of West Columbia agreed. "Who sits out in the cold, sometimes cold and rainy nights, to watch the Gamecocks do their thing? Who buys memberships in booster clubs to help get the best for USC football?

The gift from Martha Williams Brice helped South Carolina build the first upper deck on what would become Williams-Brice Stadium. The Gamecocks officially rechristened their stadium during a ceremony at halftime of the 1972 season opener. *Russell Maxey Photograph Collection, Courtesy of Richland Library, Columbia, S.C.*

We the Gamecock football boosters," he wrote. "I think we should have been asked about the change before the lawyers and politicians, better known as the board of trustees, changed the name to Williams-Brice Stadium. As usual, the lawyers and politicians…have imposed their will upon us."

But clearly those booster club donations had not been enough to help pull Carolina Stadium into the modern era. The stadium's west side—the side backing up to Bluff Road—would be the most immediate beneficiary of the Brice gift, with the $2.75 million used as part of a renovation project that included the addition of the facility's first upper deck, as well as the construction of a new press box and VIP seating area. The west side upper deck, which would increase the stadium's capacity to 56,400 seats, would be completed for the 1972 campaign.

In the meantime, there was another issue to contend with. Had the Brice gift been subject to federal estate taxes, the amount of the donation would have been reduced considerably—to around $1 million total. Led by Dietzel, the university went to work seeking political assistance and, fortunately, had at its disposal perhaps the most powerful congressional delegation the Palmetto State has ever known.

There was Representative L. Mendel Rivers, who for three decades represented the state's first congressional district in and around Charleston and was chairman of the powerful House Armed Services Committee. There was Senator Ernest "Fritz" Hollings, a former South Carolina governor who would go on to serve nearly four decades in the Senate. And there was Senator Strom Thurmond, also a former governor, who would serve forty-seven years in the Senate and hold some of the body's most powerful chairmanships. Rivers and Hollings had both attended law school at the University of South Carolina. All three legislators were influential, connected and determined to help their state's flagship university keep all of the largest private donation it had ever received.

Although Rivers would fall ill with a heart condition and pass away in the final days of 1970, he and his Senate colleagues were still able to attach a piece of special legislation to an existing excise tax bill that allowed the university to keep the total amount of Brice's donation. The lawmakers worked quickly, muscling the legislation through Congress even before the public had been made aware of the exact amount of the donation or what specifically it would be used for. "I remember Strom asked Rivers, 'How do we get this through?'" Dietzel recalled years later. "And he said, 'Well, we'll stick it in this bill, and no one will pay attention.' And that's how we got it."

For the 1971 season—in which the Gamecocks would finish a disappointing 6-5 after a starting 5-1—South Carolina's home stadium still carried its original moniker. It was on the day of the spring game the following year that the university at last confirmed the name change everyone knew was coming. A plaque bearing the Williams-Brice name had already been placed outside the stadium, and Dietzel confirmed to reporters after the exhibition that "Carolina" would be dropped completely from the stadium's name.

The change was made official during halftime of the 1972 season opener against Virginia in a ceremony that included Jones, Marchant, Thurmond, Hollings, two congressmen from the state and Martha Brice's heirs. Members of the Palmetto State's legislative delegation received thanks for their efforts in helping the university retain the full amount of the gift. It was one of the few bright spots on a night in which the Gamecocks lost, 24–16, the first defeat in what would be a 4-7 campaign. Stadium improvements were underway, but clearly the football program needed work. Despite all his efforts to modernize the football stadium, Dietzel's time at South Carolina was beginning to draw short.

Ultimately, the Williams-Brice name would appear not just on the football stadium but also on the facility hosting the university's nursing

South Carolina First District congressman L. Mendel Rivers (*left*) and Senators Strom Thurmond (*above*) and Ernest Hollings (*top left*) worked to help USC circumvent estate taxes that would have left the school with just a fraction of Martha Brice's $3.5 million gift. *Rivers, courtesy of Library of Congress Prints and Photographs Division, photograph by Warren K. Leffler; Thurmond and Hollings, courtesy of U.S. Senate Historical Office.*

college, as well as a building on the Conway campus that is now used by the athletic department at Coastal Carolina. Williams-Brice Stadium has been further expanded many times since, including the 1982 addition of an east-side upper deck—which initially swayed to an uncomfortable degree until it was reinforced—that increased capacity to 72,000. Membership in the SEC brought with it increased demands on the facility, which in 1996 was outfitted with a south end zone upper deck and suite area that boosted capacity to 80,250. From its humble roots, South Carolina's football stadium has mushroomed into the one of the twenty largest college stadiums in America, complete with a landscaped plaza and tailgating area that were completed in 2015.

From its humble beginnings as a municipal stadium built during the Great Depression, Williams-Brice Stadium has grown into an 80,250-seat facility that ranks among the twenty largest college football stadiums in America. *Courtesy of University of South Carolina Athletics.*

But the improvements made with Martha Brice's donation were what started it all. Although some athletic facilities at South Carolina are now named after corporate sponsors—most notably, the baseball stadium and basketball arena—the Gamecocks' football stadium will not follow suit. Under the terms of the agreement between the Brice estate and the university, athletic director Ray Tanner told reporters in 2015, the Williams-Brice name is guaranteed in perpetuity. As long as the Gamecocks play football in the facility at the intersection of Bluff Road and George Rogers Boulevard, they will do it at Williams-Brice Stadium.

Which is just fine to Martha Brice's ancestors. "I can't drive by the stadium without thinking about my grandfather," said Tom Brice Hall, grandson to Tom and Martha Brice. "It's an honor to have the name up there."

8

WHAT COULD HAVE BEEN

They were going to throw the slant. That much became evident to Brad Edwards when Clemson kept the tight end in, trying to protect quarterback Rodney Williams as much as possible from the relentless blitzing defense that had hounded him all night. To Edwards, the only question that remained was, which side are they throwing to? When Williams's eyes immediately tracked to the right, Edwards's side of the field, the South Carolina safety had all the information he needed. The pass never had a chance of reaching its intended target, Tigers wide receiver Keith Jennings. Edwards sat in position and then sprang, making an easy interception and returning it nearly untouched for a touchdown.

Williams-Brice Stadium had been a raucous mosh pit all night for the annual rivalry game, and the instant Edwards broke for the end zone, it exploded in a cacophony of noise. There was the jubilation of beating Clemson, with Edwards's interception with 5:37 remaining serving as the exclamation point on a 20–7 victory that wasn't as close as the final score. But for one of the most talented but snake-bitten teams in Gamecocks history, there was also the relief of finally finishing the job against a nationally ranked opponent after letting so many previous opportunities slip away.

Even all these years later, Edwards—who intercepted Williams again on the Tigers' next series—is still sent video clips of his pick-six against Clemson on almost a weekly basis. "It just speaks to the rivalry between the two institutions, and how big that is," he said. His interception on one of the more electric nights Williams-Brice has ever seen, before a national

South Carolina safety Brad Edwards (27) intercepted two passes and returned one for a touchdown in a victory over Clemson that stood as the biggest win for the Gamecocks during the 1987 season. *The State Newspaper Photograph Archive, Courtesy of Richland Library, Columbia, S.C.*

audience on ESPN, remains one of those moments that Gamecocks fans can still recall in vivid detail. But it was just one twist and turn in the 1987 season, a year full of promise and heartbreak for a South Carolina team that came so close to being the greatest ever to don the garnet and black.

It might have been hard to see that in the preseason, given that the Gamecocks were coming off a 3-6-2 campaign—their second consecutive losing record since the magical 10-2 season of 1984. And yet, there was potential for those who were able to look beyond the meager won-loss record; six times, those '86 Gamecocks had lost or tied games in which they had led in the second half, most painfully a 27–24 setback to No. 3 Nebraska in a game South Carolina had led 24–20 with five minutes remaining. Later, No. 16 North Carolina State scored with no time left to beat the Gamecocks, 23–22. South Carolina had a standout freshman quarterback in Todd Ellis, a bevy of talented skill players like receivers Sterling Sharpe and Ryan Bethea, and standout defenders like Edwards, linebacker Matt McKernan and end Kevin Hendrix. But week after week, they struggled to finish the job.

"That is probably one of the most underappreciated, probably underrated teams in that decade of major college football," Edwards said of South

Carolina's 1986 squad. "That team could have easily been a top-20 football team had just a couple of plays gone differently for them."

So, there was reason for optimism in 1987, with Ellis coming into his own as a sophomore and a solid core of experienced players on both sides of the ball. The caliber of talent that head coach Joe Morrison had assembled was an all-time high for the program and would not be surpassed until the three consecutive eleven-win seasons under Steve Spurrier from 2011 to 2013. Twelve members of the 1987 team would be drafted by NFL teams, with some players, like Sharpe, Edwards and running back Harold Green, enjoying productive pro careers. Morrison instilled his team with toughness through practices that were not for the meek. Adding to the talent level was the camaraderie built up over summer workouts, the cornerstone of what would become a tight-knit unit that was quickly able to leave adversity behind.

That resilience would be tested, in a manner that felt very familiar to those players who had suffered through all the close calls of the season before. Three games into the season, the Gamecocks traveled to No. 20 Georgia and ran up and down the field in a game in which they outgained the Bulldogs 374–231. Those final few yards before the goal line, though, proved impossible to navigate. South Carolina penetrated the Georgia 15-yard line five times. They had first-and-goal at the Bulldog 9, 7 and 2, and first downs at the 14 and 12. Yet they never made it into the end zone and were left with a headshaking 13–6 loss. One potential scoring drive was scuttled by a penalty, another by a receiver running the wrong route in the end zone, another by Georgia stripping Green of the ball at the 2 as he was straining for yardage. South Carolina's defense bottled up the Bulldogs, allowing only a Lars Tate touchdown after a short Gamecocks punt—but it proved to be the difference.

Morrison summed it up: "I don't think we had any particular problems other than the ones we created for ourselves," he told reporters afterward. Years later, Edwards still rues one that got away. "That's one we felt we should have won by 20 points," said the former Gamecock safety who would go on to become athletic director at George Mason University. "That was just a clear case of a lack of execution. You're playing Georgia and you have to give them credit, but in our minds, we just didn't execute the way we were capable of in those moments."

South Carolina still had the makings of a formidable football team, with Ellis leading a run-and-shoot offense capable of rolling up yardage and a defense that would become one of the best in the nation under the blitzing

South Carolina quarterback Todd Ellis hands off to tailback Harold Green during a game in 1987. Ellis and Green were two members of an 1987 squad that suffered several close losses to highly ranked opponents and remains among the Gamecocks' most talented squads. *The State Newspaper Photograph Archive, Courtesy of Richland Library, Columbia, S.C.*

scheme designed by first-year coordinator Joe Lee Dunn. But the Georgia loss had been an unwelcome reminder that there was still a step the Gamecocks had yet to take. And the next week, they got another one.

This time, it was Nebraska, again. Playing in Lincoln, the Gamecocks led the second-ranked Cornhuskers, 21–13, late in the third quarter and pinned them back at their own 4-yard line after a punt. Nebraska was also without starting quarterback Steve Taylor, knocked out of the game after taking a hit from Edwards and fellow safety Scott Windsor. Backup quarterback Clete Blakeman engineered a 96-yard scoring drive that cut the Gamecocks' advantage to two, and on South Carolina's ensuing possession, tailback Keith Bing fumbled after being hit on a draw play. The Huskers recovered at the Gamecocks' 27, and four plays later, Nebraska had the lead. An attempt at a late rally produced only an Ellis interception that led to another Cornhusker score.

On the scene for the *Columbia Record*, reporter Bob Gillespie wrote that "in the past two weeks, on-field memories of 1986 have come flooding back like bad TV reruns." But the Gamecocks were having none of that kind of talk. "There's no déjà vu, like we know someone's going to take the game away from us," Ellis said afterward. "They did the things to win, and that's the difference in good teams." The previous year, Morrison had overheard some of his assistants using the term "moral victory"—and he barged into the meeting room and declared that he'd fire anyone who used that phrase again. In the wake of two close, painful losses, the Gamecocks didn't wallow in what might have been. Instead, they leaned on the resiliency they had built up as a strength.

"You can look at the year before and think, 'Here we go again,' but that team did not respond that way at all," said Edwards, who played nine years in the NFL. "In fact, they responded in the exact opposite way of, 'We're a good football team, and we're going to find our way out of this. We're going to focus on that game that week, and whoever's right in front of us.' I think some of that mentality was carried forward from the Navy game from 1984—don't take anybody lightly, look only at what's in front of our face. That really helped us that year, in my view. That really played a role in building the culture of the program."

Edwards was among the seniors who had been freshmen on South Carolina's legendary 1984 team, which came out of nowhere to win 10

South Carolina receiver Sterling Sharpe set school records for receptions and receiving yards and went on to become a five-time Pro Bowl player in the NFL. *The State Newspaper Photograph Archive, Courtesy of Richland Library, Columbia, S.C.*

games and capture the hearts of Gamecock fans. But it also suffered an inexcusable loss at a 3-5-1 Navy team that likely prevented South Carolina from playing for the national championship. At a team gathering the night before the game in Annapolis, Maryland, Edwards recalls mentioning to McKernan that the team seemed to be taking the game too lightly. "I don't think we're going to play well tomorrow," he told his teammate, and they didn't. Edwards would carry the lesson from that week into the 1987 season, into the NFL and into his post-football career as an athletic administrator. "You just cannot have a down moment week-to-week," he said. "You have to bring it every single day."

The 1987 Gamecocks responded to their double dose of adversity at Georgia and Nebraska by bringing pain to the next six opponents on their schedule, winning those games by an average margin of 32 points. After a 48–0 rout of North Carolina State, South Carolina cracked the national rankings at No. 19. By the time 8th-ranked Clemson came to Columbia, the Gamecocks were No. 12. The Gamecocks' blitzing defense completely exposed the Tigers, who crossed midfield just once in the game and managed only 166 yards of total offense, the lowest output of head coach Danny Ford's tenure to that point. The result also brought immense satisfaction for a South Carolina team that had struggled to finish games against highly ranked opponents. "This is the first game we've won in two years that was close," Ellis said afterward, "and it's a great feeling for us."

The Gamecocks were rolling. They rose to No. 8 in the Associated Press poll, and the South Carolina defense—which had held its past three opponents to 36, 66 and 166 total yards, respectively—had ascended to No. 2 in the nation. Ellis was on his way to setting a school single-season passing record. But the season's ultimate challenge was still to come, in the form of a rare post-Clemson regular-season game, this one in the Orange Bowl against a brash, swaggering, undefeated Miami team loaded with future NFL All-Pros. For the Hurricanes, South Carolina represented the final step before a berth in the national championship game. For the Gamecocks, it was another shot to take down one of the nation's elite. Miami had come to Williams-Brice Stadium the season before and flexed its considerable muscle, running out to a 34–0 lead and rolling up 400 yards of offense. But the 1987 game would be very different; it would be a dogfight, in more ways than one.

Edwards had been ill on the flight down from Columbia, spending the entire trip vomiting in the aircraft lavatory. His first snap of the game was a wake-up call—he was lined up one-on-one defending Michael Irvin in the

South Carolina coach Joe Morrison fielded his most talented team in 1987, although the Gamecocks would finish 8-4 against a schedule that featured five ranked opponents. *The State Newspaper Photograph Archive, Courtesy of Richland Library, Columbia, S.C.*

slot. South Carolina's trademark blitz went after Hurricanes quarterback Steve Walsh, who checked off on almost every play and picked apart the Gamecocks' man-to-man coverage. Looking back, Edwards wondered if South Carolina should have employed a zone. But South Carolina's system had worked for much of the season, and they stuck with it, and Walsh took advantage by passing for a career-high 310 yards.

The Hurricanes set the tone early when Walsh connected with Irvin for a 46-yard touchdown, but the Gamecocks were within 1 at halftime after Ellis hit Sharpe with a short pass that the receiver turned into a 47-yard score. In the third quarter, Miami unleashed another big play, this time between Walsh and Brian Blades for 56 yards and a touchdown. "At some point, you have only so much gas in the tank," Edwards recalled. Meanwhile, the atmosphere had a tension to it, with Miami's brashness infusing the entire Orange Bowl and South Carolina taking a cue from its tough, never-back-down head coach. Hendrix remembers plenty of trash talking and extra licks after the play, and lots of verbal abuse coming from fans in the stands. "We knew it was coming sooner or later," he said. And with nine minutes left in the game, it erupted.

The spark was Miami defensive end Daniel Stubbs, who charged around the right side on a play that was blown dead by a whistle for an offsides penalty. Ellis slowed his drop-back and extended his arm, trying to signal that the play was over. But Stubbs kept coming, dragging Ellis backward 10 yards and slamming the quarterback to the turf. The Gamecocks' offensive line went after Stubbs, pile-driving him into the ground. "It was pretty much chaos after that," recalled Ellis, who would become the radio play-by-play voice of Gamecocks football. South Carolina's sideline emptied, with players not in the game strapping on helmets before charging into the melee. "We knew…they were going to try to bully us," Hendrix said. "We were ready to go."

Nationally, the fracas came to define the game, somewhat overshadowing the performance the Gamecocks had shown against an opponent that would go on to win the national championship. But in the end, Miami was just too much. On the first play after the melee ended—with no ejections and officials even forgetting to assess the Hurricanes offsides that had blown the play dead—Ellis was intercepted. The Gamecocks had one last shot from their own 12 with 2:37 left, but a fourth-down pass sailed over the head of receiver Danny Smith and onto the South Carolina sideline, and the Hurricanes' hard-fought 20–16 victory was finally secure.

South Carolina quarterback Todd Ellis passed for a school record 3,206 yards in the 1987 season, a mark that stood until it was eclipsed by Dylan Thompson in 2014. *The State Newspaper Photograph Archive, Courtesy of Richland Library, Columbia, S.C.*

South Carolina receiver Sterling Sharpe celebrates with fans at Williams-Brice Stadium after a victory in 1987. That team contained the Gamecocks' greatest assemblage of talent until Steve Spurrier led the program to three consecutive 11-win seasons from 2011 to 2013. *The State Newspaper Photograph Archive, Courtesy of Richland Library, Columbia, S.C.*

For the 1987 Gamecocks, it was another case of what might have been. They lost three games that regular season, all on the road, against opponents ranked No. 20, No. 2 and No. 2, by a combined total of 20 points. Their Gator Bowl appearance against No. 7 LSU proved anticlimactic and underwhelming—with a month to prepare, the Tigers were more than ready for South Carolina's blitzing defense, and they picked it apart in a 30–13 victory. The Gamecocks' 8-4 final record that season gives very little indication of just how stacked with talent that squad was and how differently the season might have turned out with a touchdown against Georgia and a few timely defensive stops against Nebraska and Miami.

And yet, to the players on that team and others who remember it, the 1987 squad has more than earned its place among the greatest Gamecock squads of all time. Other teams finished with better records—but few were as talented or went up against as difficult a schedule. Beyond 1984 and the three eleven-win Spurrier teams, "you have to look at '87 as that next year with respect to not only what happened, but what could have been," Edwards said. "Even if you take the latter part of that, what could have been, and get into a true examination of what happened on the field and the kind of opponents that you played, it does elevate it. But it takes that kind of contextual examination to do that."

9

STEROIDS AND SCANDAL

The stack of papers handed to Joe Morrison numbered more than a dozen, but the South Carolina football coach needed only to glance at the first few for the reality of the situation to sink in. Sports information director Kerry Tharp had brought to Morrison's office an advance copy of an exposé on the Gamecocks soon to be published by *Sports Illustrated* and braced himself for the reaction from the man in black.

"Coach," Tharp told him, "you need to read this."

What followed was an angry, profane outburst from a coach whose program would soon be mired in a scandal involving what in 1988 was still a relatively little-known issue: performance-enhancing steroids. It was one of the first signs of the coming plague that would eventually sweep through all sports, leading to stripped Olympic medals, tainted baseball home-run chases, broken bodies and vacated athletic accomplishments. But steroid use at the time was a much lesser-known phenomenon, and within South Carolina, the *Sports Illustrated* story went off like a bomb.

Understandably so. In the late 1980s, ESPN was a still-growing network in barely half of all American households with televisions, and the internet was a nascent form of computer communication used primarily by research facilities, universities and government agencies. For a major college sports team of the time, few media outlets packed the punch of *Sports Illustrated*, which then offered an almost unrivaled degree of national reach. News moved so slowly, and the magazine, published weekly, was so relevant, that even its days-later game recaps still felt vivid. As a result, universities coveted the prospect of being featured in the pages of *SI*.

Except for South Carolina in the fall of 1988. The sheaf of paper Tharp handed Morrison contained an explosive, first-person account by former Gamecocks defensive lineman Tommy Chaikin cowritten by Rick Telander alleging widespread steroid use within the South Carolina football program. The fourteen-page story, accompanied by lurid illustrations, was entitled "The Nightmare of Steroids" and opened with a paragraph many in the Palmetto State can still recite by heart: "I was sitting in my room at the Roost, the athletic dorm at the University of South Carolina, with a loaded .357 Magnum pressed under my chin."

Now, just Chaikin's accounts of players being pushed to the brink of heat exhaustion during practice—he recalled collapsing in a huddle and Morrison chiding anyone who sought shade from the unforgiving Columbia summer sun—would be enough to spark an inquiry. Chaikin's claims of rampant steroid use at South Carolina painted a picture of an out-of-control program awash in guns, vials, pills and syringes, and a coaching staff that allegedly turned a blind eye to it all. The Gamecocks were instantly colored as an outlaw program reflective of the all-black outfits that Morrison favored on the sideline. "It's tainted us," athletic director King Dixon said in the aftermath. "It's had a tremendous adverse effect as far as what people think of us."

By his junior year, Chaikin wrote in the *SI* piece, he surmised that half of the players on the Gamecock squad were using steroids. He had become not just a user but also a supplier to many of his teammates in the locker room. Hooked on performance enhancers that jacked his weight from 210 to 235 and his bench press by 200 pounds, the Bethesda, Maryland native went through one drug after another: human growth hormone, rhesus monkey hormone, anabolic steroids of various kinds, testosterone, even a type of horse steroid. By his senior year, he wrote, he was taking two testosterone injections every third day and swallowing ten tablets of steroids daily.

The effects soon became evident in more than just his physique. Chaikin wrote in *SI* that he developed acne, an elevated heart rate, sleeplessness, chest pain, a swollen liver, numbness and benign tumors that needed to be surgically removed. His anxiety grew so bad, he said, that he began seeing a psychiatrist and taking antidepressants. But more than anything, there was the rage. He had become "one of the meanest guys on the team," and his outbursts became more and more violent: he said he became involved in bar fights that would leave others unconscious, he ripped a locker off its hinges, he destroyed a refrigerator with a baseball bat and he even pulled a shotgun on a pizza delivery man.

It all cast South Carolina in a terrible light, especially given that Chaikin claims that team doctors and assistant coaches looked the other way and made little attempt to curb the steroid problem within the program. Morrison's lone admonishment, he wrote, was "don't do it anymore." A former NFL player, Morrison was painted as being a rather removed head coach who didn't ask many questions of his players and, when made aware of Chaikin's steroid use, was allegedly more concerned with leaks to the news media. When Chaikin finally left school following his breakdown with the .357 Magnum before the Clemson game of his senior year—saved by his father banging on his dorm room door, he said, and whisking him away to a hospital near his hometown—reports at the time said only that he was suffering from "a mysterious illness."

There were repercussions on and off the field. Six months before the *SI* exposé, South Carolina had fired its former athletic director,

A former star player at South Carolina, King Dixon took the reins as Gamecock athletic director at a turbulent time that saw the program trying to escape the shadow of a steroid scandal. *The State Newspaper Photograph Archive, Courtesy of Richland Library, Columbia, S.C.*

Bob Marcum, alleging shortcomings in the athletic program's drug-testing program—which Chaikin attests to, claiming in the *SI* piece that players routinely filled their sample cups from vials of untainted urine. After Marcum's successor resigned six months later due to health reasons, the university called on Dixon, the straightlaced former U.S. Marine and Gamecock football star, to try and clean everything up. Chaikin was threatened with criminal prosecution by a South Carolina solicitor before receiving immunity for testifying to the veracity of his claims in the story. *Sports Illustrated* paid his legal fees, which were a reported $20,000.

The drama extended from the football field to the courtroom. After the *SI* story appeared, an existing investigation by the South Carolina Law Enforcement Division into steroid distribution was expanded into a federal probe. Four assistants at South Carolina—defensive line coach James Washburn, tight end coach Thomas Kurucz, defensive coordinator Thomas Gadd and strength and conditioning coach Keith Kephart—were indicted by a grand jury in connection with steroid distribution to players. Washburn, Kurucz and Gadd were accused of conspiring to provide money to certain players and personnel for the purchase of steroids; Kephart was charged with administering the drugs.

Covering the story for *The State* newspaper in Columbia, Bob Gillespie heard one denial after another from members of the football staff. "You could sort of tell there was something there, though," he recalled, remembering how many of the staffers who would later go on trial "were extremely upset and nervous."

Over time, information began to leak out. Three former South Carolina players told the *Charlotte (NC) Observer* newspaper that Chaikin's claims were "pretty accurate" and "there was a lot of pressure to take [steroids]." Former offensive lineman Woody Myers told the paper he had used steroids "and would use them again." Players still with the Gamecocks at the time told *The State* that steroid use among Chaikin and those in his circle "was no big secret," although they stopped short of directly implicating coaches.

Morrison himself professed no knowledge of steroid use under his watch, a statement he believed was backed up by the fact that only one Gamecock player had tested positive for steroids when the team had been subjected to an NCAA drug test prior to appearing in the Gator Bowl the season before. But Gillespie unearthed a key piece of evidence in an interview with Kephart, who said he noticed some linemen struggling with running drills due to water retention during one workout in 1985.

"Coach," Kephart said he was told by the players, "we think there may be a problem with this particular chemical."

That chemical was the steroid Anadrol-50. Kephart said he told the linemen to stop using and then reported the incident to Morrison. "He said if there was anything he needed to do, to let him know. But after that, it didn't come up again," Kephart told Gillespie. He added that Morrison, an old-school coach reared in the ways of the NFL, "doesn't know anything about steroids. On the Woody (Myers) thing…he's still naive about that."

Washburn, Kephart and Kurucz pleaded guilty to charges that at the time were considered misdemeanors. A federal judge sentenced Kurucz to six months in a halfway house and three years' probation, while Washburn and Kephart were each sentenced to three months in a halfway house and given three-year probation. Gadd fought the charges against him; after two hours of deliberation, a jury in a U.S. District Court found him not guilty on both counts, a fact that Gillespie said led the other staff members involved "to smack themselves in the head for pleading out." The assistants struggled to find work in football afterward, with the exception of Washburn, who briefly served under former Clemson coach Danny Ford at Arkansas before finding a home in the NFL.

Prosecutors chose not to pursue charges against any players, viewing them as victims in the case. Chaikin resettled in his native Maryland, where he went into business, raised a family and tried to move on from the controversy that had swirled around him while at South Carolina. "I was young and didn't understand the ramifications of opening my mouth to the press," he told the Associated Press in 2005. Since then, "I guess I've been reluctant to talk about it."

Meanwhile, South Carolina embarked on a campaign to rebrand its football program and athletic department, beginning with a move to garnet uniforms—a departure from the primarily black togs that had been a hallmark of Morrison's tenure but in too many minds had become connected with steroids and scandal. The school even subtly distanced itself from the script "Carolina" logo Morrison wore on his black ball caps, instead emphasizing the program's more traditional "Block C" insignia. In the 2018 season, the Gamecocks brought back the script logo under head coach Will Muschamp, even featuring it on helmets for the first time. The following year, South Carolina fully re-embraced the "Black Magic" era by wearing 1987 throwback uniforms for several games.

The football program itself escaped damage when, in 1990, the NCAA ruled that South Carolina had done enough to remove those responsible for the steroid scandal. The university had submitted to the NCAA a four-hundred-page internal investigation that found "widespread experimentation" with steroids within the football program from 1983 to 1987, and later took part in a hearing before members of the NCAA's Committee on Infractions in Kansas City. In parts of the investigation released to the media after multiple outlets filed Freedom of Information Act requests, Kephart again proved key. Morrison and the staff "had to know or they were blind," he said in the investigation, adding, "there was an attitude of, nothing is going to happen to you if you're caught."

As for the man charged with overseeing the football team? His potential culpability in the disrepute coloring his program will never truly be known—three months after the publication of the *SI* story, in February 1989, Morrison collapsed in a shower at Williams-Brice Stadium and died of a heart attack. The U.S. attorney prosecuting the assistant coaches in the aftermath did not answer questions as to whether he believed Morrison had knowledge of the widespread steroid use within his locker room. Had Morrison lived, many believe the scandal under his watch had so tarnished the university that his time at South Carolina would have been at an end.

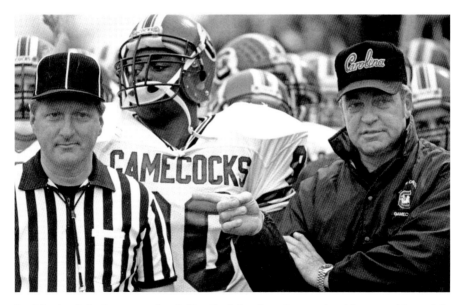

Joe Morrison's final season as South Carolina's head coach was tainted by a steroid scandal that led the university to move away from many of the colors and logos that had been associated with that era. *The State Newspaper Photograph Archive, Courtesy of Richland Library, Columbia, S.C.*

"He felt there was an effort to get him out of there," Marcum, the former athletic director, recalled years later. "He told me, 'I think it's time for me to get out of here. I'll probably take an NFL assistant's job.' Joe never defined what he was talking about, but the level of cooperation had started to erode."

Morrison had certainly clashed with Dixon, even before the steroid scandal arose. A paternity suit against the Gamecocks' coach had embarrassed the university in Dixon's view, and the athletic director bristled when he found beer in the minifridge in the head football coach's office while showing around a prospective candidate for the job. No surprise, then, that the man Dixon chose to succeed Morrison was Phillip "Sparky" Woods, a young, fresh-faced coach who had enjoyed success at lower-level Appalachian State.

But it was an uphill battle; Woods inherited a program that saw both season-ticket sales and recruiting take a hit in the wake of the scandal, and the program entered the rough-and-tumble SEC before it truly possessed the manpower or facilities to compete. The Gamecocks lost a number of signees in the scandal's aftermath, and Woods faced an additional challenge in that Morrison's death came just three days before the opening of the national signing period. The new coach signed just one player. "There's no doubt recruiting has been hurt because of the scandal," Woods said at the time. "We'll suffer now, and we'll suffer in the future because of it."

For a South Carolina football program that had enjoyed precious few of them up to that point, the Morrison era delivered starved fans one gridiron high after another: the "Black Magic" of the storied 1984 season that had the Gamecocks one unthinkable victory from perhaps challenging for the national championship; 1987's raucous victory over Clemson; triumphs over established college football bluebloods like Southern California and Notre Dame; a feeling that, at last, the Gamecocks had arrived. And suddenly, it was all a memory. The 1988 season opened with six straight wins and ended with South Carolina's third bowl berth in Morrison's final five seasons. The Gamecocks wouldn't go to another bowl game until 1994.

And yet, if there is the narrowest of silver linings to be found amid one of South Carolina's darkest chapters, it is that the steroid scandal and the end of the Morrison era showed how badly the Gamecocks' athletic administration was in need of modernization. Dixon had been a former star player at South Carolina, and his love for his alma mater knew no bounds; but the former U.S. Marine and bank executive had no previous experience in athletic administration, and his nearly two-month-long search for a head basketball coach set a standard for futility. "No offense, but Dixon wasn't qualified to run a large program like that," said David Newton, a former Gamecock beat writer for *The State*. South Carolina's athletic facilities were aging, and after years as an independent, the school's entry into the SEC was an eye-opener in more ways than one.

It would take better development, better facilities and more professional administration to get the Gamecocks where they wanted to go. Help would be on the way in the form of future athletic directors Mike McGee and Eric Hyman, who played central roles in ushering the Gamecocks into a more modern age. While it may have been difficult to envision it in the midst of scandal in 1988, South Carolina's greatest days were still to come.

10

THE REAL THING

He swung imaginary baseball bats to hit imaginary home runs, scribbled an invisible signature on the logo at midfield and spread his arms wide as if welcoming the chaos that was erupting all around him. Most of the 83,500 spectators in attendance on that Saturday afternoon were in a sour mood already, given the soggy conditions and the events unfolding on the field. And now here was this brash, young, long-haired quarterback reveling in it all. The loathing of the home fans in Clemson's Memorial Stadium cascaded down, falling even harder than the rain. Steve Taneyhill devoured it all with unabashed glee.

"The energy in the stadium that day was unbelievable," Taneyhill remembered years later. "Honestly, I was just having fun. The home run swings, we set all that up. We talked about having some fun with that. Standing at the Tiger paw and raising my hands, that was very spontaneous."

Even today, Clemson fans rue and South Carolina fans celebrate the events of that 1992 afternoon in Death Valley, when the Gamecocks' charismatic freshman quarterback turned the Palmetto State's biggest rivalry on its ear. The 24–13 upset was South Carolina's first victory at Clemson in eight years and served as an exclamation point to a rousing charge through the second half of that season. The catalyst to it all was Taneyhill, whose trademark ponytail and phenomenal touch on the football enraptured much of the state. He would finish his career as one of the most accomplished passers in program history, but in many minds, Taneyhill still stands tall for that one triumphant moment behind enemy lines.

If only getting to that point had been as effortless as South Carolina's ambush of Clemson seemed on that wet November day. The Gamecocks lost their first five games of that 1992 campaign and at one point owned the longest active losing streak in major-college football. Within the locker room ran an undercurrent of dissention, as players who had been recruited by former coach Joe Morrison chafed under their new head coach, Sparky Woods. At midseason, the frustration level grew so high that a number of players demanded Woods's resignation—a moment that in South Carolina is still known simply as the player revolt.

Then there was Taneyhill, a prized recruit from the quarterback hotbed of western Pennsylvania who opened the season as a third-stringer and played only sparingly over a first half in which the Gamecocks struggled not only to win games but also just to score. At one point, the 1992 Gamecocks were 0-5, averaging just over 9 points per game and in open mutiny against their head coach. The program's inaugural season in the mighty Southeastern Conference was becoming an embarrassment and on the brink of spiraling completely out of control.

And suddenly, everything changed. The weekend after the player revolt, the Gamecocks upset a Mississippi State team ranked 15th nationally for the program's first victory since October of the previous season. Then they won four of their next five games, knocking off another nationally ranked opponent in the process (No. 16 Tennessee) before upsetting Clemson to end a four-game losing streak in the rivalry. While they didn't go to a bowl game—an oh-so-close loss at No. 11 Florida left them one victory shy of the six wins needed for postseason qualification—they still engineered one of the biggest turnarounds in the nation and seemed to place the program on solid footing for the years to come.

The reason was Taneyhill, whose cocksure demeanor instilled needed confidence within a beaten-down locker room and whose passing ability reinvigorated an offense that had lost its way. He took over a winless football team, received his first start just days after the player revolt and still lost only one game the rest of the way. In the history of Gamecock football, few six-game spans were as magical, or as surprising.

"It was the swagger with which Taneyhill played that brought excitement and hope to the program," recalled David Newton, who covered that season for *The State* newspaper of Columbia. "He would pull out his imaginary six-shooters and fire them after a big play or touchdown. He would run around the sideline waving a white towel to rev up the fans. He was just different, down to his ponytail. The team just needed a change, and his arrival was like the perfect storm. The confidence he brought to the offense carried over to the rest of the offense, team, and ultimately the fans. He just brought an energy to the table that was much-needed. He wasn't Joe Namath predicting a Super Bowl victory, but it almost felt the same."

As that season began, though, Taneyhill was mired deep in the depth chart and had peeved some of his new South Carolina teammates by telling a reporter the previous spring that he planned to start—as a true freshman—that following season. Instead, it was senior Wright Mitchell who started the much-anticipated inaugural SEC contest against No. 14 Georgia, and the final result was a 28–6 loss that served as a preview of what was to come. Mitchell and redshirt freshman Blake Williamson would rotate starts though the first five games, but in either case, the product was the same: a Gamecocks offense that scored in double digits just once, that in a 20–18 loss to East Carolina.

After opening his freshman season as third-string quarterback, Steve Taneyhill became starter in the middle of the 1992 campaign and led the Gamecocks to five wins in their final six games. Over a storied career, he set numerous passing records and led South Carolina to its first bowl victory in 1995. *Courtesy of the* Post and Courier, *Charleston, S.C.*

At times over the first half of that season, with two quarterbacks ahead of him, Taneyhill had been reduced to running the scout team—a task he struggled with. "I didn't even know how to do that, really, because I played defense in high school," he recalled. "I played free safety, so when the scout team was going, I was on the other side. I'll be the first to tell you, I wasn't very good at it."

Even Taneyhill's debut was inauspicious. Inserted during what would become a 45–7 blowout at the hands of Arkansas, his first pass attempt in a South Carolina uniform was intercepted and returned for a touchdown. For a player who had chosen South Carolina over mighty Alabama in large part due to the prospect of immediate playing time—the Crimson Tide already had a likely starter in Jay Barker—the sitting, waiting and only occasional doses of playing time were difficult to take.

"It was frustrating, because I knew I could help," Taneyhill remembered. "And it was frustrating because I had never sat the bench in any sport. A lot of college football players go through that same thing—you're always the star in high school and junior high, and you get to college as a freshman, and you're at the back of the line. But it was very frustrating to me because our defense played good enough for us to win, and we just couldn't do anything on offense. I wasn't used to being that relief pitcher. I needed to play. The starting quarterback, you're in a leadership role just because of the position. Backup quarterback, you're not. It was just very frustrating to sit and not be out there as the starter. And I thought if I could just get out there and be the guy who started the game, I could help."

Taneyhill moved up to second on the depth chart when Mitchell quit the team after losing the starting job. In a blowout loss at an Alabama team that would go on to win the national championship, Taneyhill received his first extensive playing time of the season and completed 10 of 17 passes for 135 yards. With an off week next, Taneyhill flew home to Altoona, Pennsylvania—and found himself on the same flight as Gamecocks assistant Rich Bisaccia, who was heading to western Pennsylvania to recruit. "He told me I was going to start," Taneyhill recalled, "but I couldn't tell anybody." His debut as starting quarterback would come the following weekend, when the 0-5 Gamecocks hosted No. 15 Mississippi State.

Taneyhill returned to Columbia that Sunday ready to prepare for his first start—only to see the early part of the week thrown into chaos by teammates who demanded Woods's dismissal. Days earlier, Woods had told *The State* that South Carolina's woes resulted in part from poor recruiting in the final two years of Morrison's tenure—given that only sixteen of forty-three players signed over that period were still with the program, and just five were listed as starters. The effect of that attrition, Woods told the newspaper, was "like getting the death penalty," comparing it to the severe form of NCAA punishment that shuts down a program and prohibits recruiting for a given period of time.

For Woods, there was frustration apart from the losing. In his fourth season, he had yet to take the Gamecocks to a bowl game, even though his first two teams had qualified with 6-5 records. Athletic director King Dixon, Newton recalled, turned down Independence Bowl invitations both years because the date of the game conflicted with the school's exam schedule. "Since the school still was coming off the steroid scandal, there was a lot of pressure to make the student part of student-athlete important to put the seemingly win-at-all-costs attitude of the Joe Morrison days in the rearview mirror," added Newton, who later joined ESPN. "Sparky was confident one or both of those six-win teams would have ended the school's bowl futility, and always felt that hurt his recruiting efforts."

A three-win season the previous year—which included two ties and a loss at East Carolina, after which Pirates fans tore down the goal posts—had everyone on edge before the 1992 campaign even began. Within the locker room, the few remaining holdovers from the Morrison era still revered their former head coach, and they took Woods's comments about Morrison's recruiting as a personal affront. The result was a team meeting before practice that Monday, in which a reported sixty-two of ninety-six players voted in favor of Woods resigning. When Woods walked in on the meeting, he was asked to leave, and the results of the vote were posted on the blackboard. "A lot of players on this team don't respect him. I don't respect him. It's hard to play for somebody you don't respect," one anonymous player told Newton. Woods later said one player told him directly, "We want you to resign."

Newton was trying to get his newborn son to sleep that night when the phone rang. The call was from a Gamecocks player whom Newton trusted, tipping him off to news of the revolt. The beat writer called other players, who confirmed the meeting and the vote of no confidence in their head coach, then tried to confirm with Woods and members of the board of trustees. "I eventually made my way to the stadium which was about 20 minutes from home, but by then nobody was around," he recalled. "I kept in touch with players throughout the evening, and when I finally went to bed, there remained uncertainty over whether they would show up for practice or whether Woods would remain the coach."

Looking back, Taneyhill believes the revolt was "blown out of proportion." Even so, he recalls heading to practice the next day and seeing what looked like fifty television crews waiting on the team to arrive. "I think the seniors just weren't happy with a few things," he remembered. "It was all a big cloud and foggy to me, because my mind is on, this is my first start. I just went along. I couldn't focus on [the player revolt], because I had to get myself ready to play. That was my main thing that week—getting ready to play, and getting into that game plan as much as I could. As a freshman, and I hadn't played that much, it's not scary, but it's a different dynamic that week leading to being a starter. I was anxious, but nervous at the same time."

While some hard feelings remained—"I don't see how people can just forget about it overnight. A lot of players felt we needed a change," linebacker Konata Reid said—by the next day, an uneasy truce had taken hold. There had been no dismissals, and no players had quit, Woods told reporters. Everyone had reported for 10:00 a.m. position meetings. University president John Palms met with players in the locker room before practice, assuring them that everyone understood their frustration. "When your team is on a losing streak like that," Newton said, "everyone is looking for answers."

Amid the upheaval, the fact that Taneyhill had been taking first-team practice reps for a week went largely overlooked. While news of the freshman's first start was still unknown to the public—Woods wouldn't officially announce his starter for Mississippi State until the Thursday before the game—within the locker room, it had become well known that a change of starting quarterback was underway. Taneyhill recalls numerous teammates stopping by his dorm room, rooting him on. "When you're 0-5 and the whole team is down," he said, "anything that sparks your momentum is going to be seen as a positive."

Long before he arrived at South Carolina, Taneyhill had developed a reputation for engineering dramatic turnarounds. He joined a Little League team that went 3-27 his first season and then won consecutive local championships. In fourth grade, his flag football team won three area titles. In high school, he led the basketball team to its first trip to the state finals in twenty-seven years. But the 1992 Gamecocks were his masterwork, and the result was the greatest in-season reversal in program history. With Taneyhill behind center, the Gamecocks were a different team, generating a season-high 505 yards of total offense in a 21–6 victory over Mississippi State that released the tension built up within the team like air escaping from a balloon.

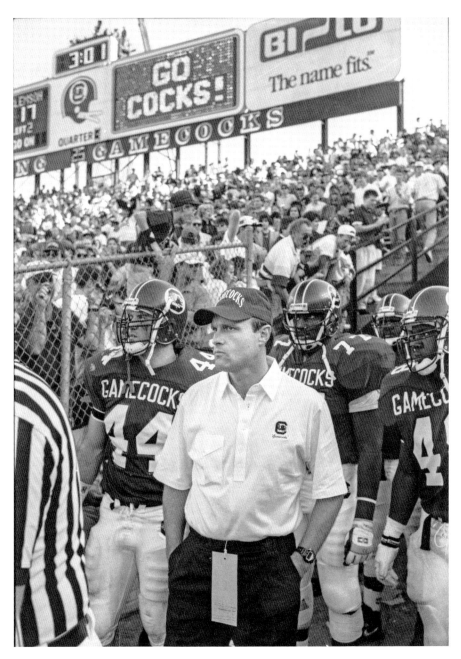

Succeeding the late Joe Morrison as South Carolina head coach was Sparky Woods, who faced not only recruiting fallout from the steroid scandal but also entry into the rugged SEC. And during a winless first half to the 1992 campaign, several upperclassmen players demanded his resignation. *The State Newspaper Photograph Archive, Courtesy of Richland Library, Columbia, S.C.*

"I'm a believer now," tight end Boomer Foster told reporters after the game. "He's said a lot of stuff in the papers, but he's the real thing."

It was just the beginning. The next week, the Gamecocks rallied from 14–0 down to win at Vanderbilt, where Williamson rushed for the winning score after Taneyhill took a hit on his throwing arm and left the game. He was well enough to throw two touchdown passes the following Saturday, as South Carolina twice rallied from behind and walk-on linebacker Hank Campbell stopped Tennessee's attempt at a go-ahead two-point conversion with 1:28 left as the Gamecocks stunned the No. 16 Volunteers, 24–23. The only hiccup during that second-half run came at reigning SEC champion Florida, where the Gamecocks led 3–0 at halftime but allowed two late scores to fall, 14–9.

Taneyhill's confidence became contagious, rubbing off on everyone associated with the program. "I just think as the quarterback, if you show that you have faith in your own ability and that you trust your teammates and their abilities, obviously confidence grows," he said. "We had confidence in each other, especially after that first win."

The capper to it all was the victory at Clemson, in a rivalry game whose magnitude Taneyhill admits he didn't fully understand until he played in it for the first time. After a winless first half to the season, a player revolt and then a stirring turnaround, winning at Death Valley was "icing on the cake," Taneyhill said. Although Taneyhill would develop into one of the most accomplished passers in South Carolina history—he threw for over 3,000 yards as a senior in 1995, including a program single-game record 473 yards at Mississippi State—the promise of that 5-1 finish in 1992 would not be realized immediately. The Gamecocks stumbled to 4-7 the next year, costing Woods his job. The breakthrough would not come until 1994 under first-year head coach Brad Scott, when Taneyhill and South Carolina won seven games—their highest total in six years—and earned the program's first bowl victory.

But the second half of that 1992 campaign remains a vivid, joyous experience to those who remember it. Taneyhill became a folk hero, with fans buying caps that featured a ponytail dangling from the back. Later a successful high school coach, Taneyhill became owner of a tavern in the Five Points area of Columbia—where fans still regularly approach him about 1992. Even Woods, the once-beleaguered and eventually ousted head coach, is able to look back fondly on how that season marred by a player mutiny produced a six-game stretch that remains cherished today.

"Sometimes in crisis, people pull together," he said years later. "I saw it as a real positive. It showed the value of teamwork."

Things hardly seemed that rosy early on, as dissention brewed among upperclassmen recruited by another coach and Taneyhill languished on the practice squad. Back in those frustrating first weeks defined by one lopsided loss after another, could he dare to foresee such a dramatic turn of events? "I don't know that we ever thought we could do it at the beginning," Taneyhill remembered. "But I think every Saturday when we took the field after that first victory, we thought we were going to win."

TURNING THE TIDE

A mid the celebratory din of nearly eighty-three thousand rapturous fans at Williams-Brice Stadium, the two starting quarterbacks shared a moment at midfield. "We'll see y'all again," Alabama's Greg McElroy told his South Carolina counterpart, Stephen Garcia, in reference to the SEC Championship Game two months away. It was a rare, fleeting point in time—one in which a star-crossed Gamecocks outfit stood shoulder-to-shoulder with the best college football program in America, and the quarterback of the defending national champions offered coded congratulations to a signal-caller who had been benched in his previous game.

But such neck-snapping extremes were the norm for Garcia. Off the field, he had a penchant for getting into the kind of trouble that jeopardized not only his status with the football program but also his standing within the university. On the field, he could sometimes leave head coach Steve Spurrier tossing his play sheet in frustration or bent over with his hands on his knees. But the quarterback was also capable of delivering moments so spectacular that they continue to live on in South Carolina football lore. The biggest of those came in October 2010, when Garcia played the game of his career in leading the Gamecocks to their biggest victory in school history: a 35–21 humbling of top-ranked Alabama—indeed, the Alabama of Bear Bryant and Nick Saban and all those national titles—which came to Columbia riding a winning streak of twenty-nine straight regular-season games.

Spurrier was never one to heap praise on his junior quarterback, given the often-strained relationship between the two. But after Garcia completed seventeen of twenty passes for 201 yards and three touchdowns to beat the Crimson Tide, Spurrier—known to college football fans as the "Head Ball Coach"—couldn't help himself. "He was sensational," Spurrier said. Garcia even overcame his one real gaffe—giving up a safety on the first play of the second half by tossing a bad snap deep in his own territory off the goal post, a move that led to five straight Alabama points and had Gamecocks fans suddenly shifting nervously in their seats. But he made up for it by engineering a fifteen-play, 82-yard scoring drive that took nearly eight minutes off the clock. The mighty Crimson Tide never threatened again.

It was a day notable for so many reasons. The final result marked the first time South Carolina had ever beaten the nation's No. 1 team in football. It was the biggest win for the Gamecocks since a victory over No. 3 North Carolina in 1981, and it was just the program's third win against a top-five team in thirty-seven attempts. And but for one moment early in the second half, it was a game that South Carolina completely controlled, with the two-touchdown margin of victory making the contest look closer than it really was. And it might never have happened, had Garcia made some different decisions earlier in his South Carolina career, or had Spurrier chosen a different starting quarterback in the days before the game.

Two weeks earlier, Garcia's status as starter was shaky at best, and the idea that the Gamecocks could handle No. 1 Alabama seemed about as unlikely as Spurrier riding a rocket to the moon. Questions about the quarterback position dogged South Carolina coming out of its previous game at Auburn, where the Gamecocks had given up a six-point lead early in the fourth quarter and were left with a 35–27 defeat. The source of the meltdown was not difficult to pinpoint: four turnovers on as many possessions in the fourth quarter, two of them fumbles committed by Garcia when he was scrambling to pick up yardage. As a result, he was benched with six minutes to play and could only watch as a true freshman backup named Connor Shaw was intercepted twice inside the Auburn 15-yard line.

"We should have won," Garcia told reporters after the game. "Turnovers in the second half just killed us."

In the immediate aftermath, Spurrier made no pronouncements about his starting quarterback. With an open date between the Auburn loss and the Alabama game, the head coach could afford to take his time. Garcia, though, anticipated that he'd have to perform in practice to keep the job. "I expect that," he said underneath Auburn's Jordan-Hare Stadium. "I expected that when (Shaw) got here in the spring."

At the time, Shaw seemed something of a project—a three-star recruit out of high school who had graduated early in order to take part in spring practice before his freshman season. Shaw didn't draw much interest from other schools in the SEC, choosing the Gamecocks over Georgia Tech, East Carolina, Stanford, Wake Forest and West Virginia. Although the son of a coach, there were few indications that he would blossom into the greatest quarterback in South Carolina history, leading the program to an unprecedented three straight eleven-win seasons. It was Garcia, a four-star prospect rated by the recruiting service Rivals as the fourth-best high school quarterback nationally, who was viewed as the savior. When Garcia committed to the Gamecocks in December 2006—over the likes of Oklahoma, Auburn and Florida—it was easy to believe that the quarterback maestro Spurrier had found his first great quarterback at South Carolina.

But there were immediate hiccups. One month after he enrolled early, Garcia was arrested for an alcohol-related infraction. He'd go on to have three run-ins with the law in fifteen months, one for allegedly keying the car of a visiting professor, another a citation for underage drinking. Hours after that latter offense, he was referred to the university's student disciplinary system for allegedly discharging a fire extinguisher. Garcia completed pretrial intervention to have two of the charges wiped from his record, while a third charge was dropped. But the university was tiring of Garcia's antics, taking any disciplinary measures out of Spurrier's hands.

"They've got a president. They've got an athletic director. They've got a dean. They've got a whole bunch of people over there," Spurrier said in March 2008. "So if they say he's here, he'll be here, OK? His fate is out of my hands. Let's put it that way."

The university's reaction was to suspend Garcia not just from the football program but also from school until that August, prohibiting him from taking summer classes at South Carolina or participating in any team activities. He returned to his parents' home outside Tampa, Florida, where he complied with conditions that included keeping a summer job, performing community service and providing updates to university officials about his progress. By all accounts, he was a model citizen, and his good behavior allowed him to return to South Carolina two weeks earlier than scheduled, which enabled him to participate in all of preseason camp for the 2008 campaign.

All of that drama occurred before Garcia had even played his first game wearing garnet and black, a moment that didn't come until three games into his redshirt freshman season of 2008. Garcia made a brief appearance in a loss to Georgia in relief of starter Chris Smelley, and he received a huge ovation from the fans at Williams-Brice Stadium, who had longed to see their prized quarterback recruit in action. "I'm glad they still like me after everything that I've been through," he quipped afterward.

His first start came five weeks later in a loss to LSU, and from there it was a roller coaster. There was the moment before bowl bids were announced when Spurrier named Garcia the starter over Smelley, who would soon transfer to Alabama to play baseball. There was the ugly 31–10 Outback Bowl loss to Iowa—in Garcia's hometown of Tampa—after which Spurrier complained that his quarterback had spent too much time playing golf and video games and catching up with friends rather than studying the playbook. There was the summer during which Spurrier repeatedly questioned Garcia's commitment level and conditioning. There was a 2010 preseason camp in which Spurrier opened the quarterback competition between Garcia and the freshman Shaw.

And yet, there were also unforgettable moments that reminded everyone of what Garcia was capable of while on the field. In October 2008, he came off the bench and tossed a fourth-quarter touchdown pass to Weslye Saunders to rally the Gamecocks past Kentucky. In September 2009, he threw a 2-yard touchdown pass to fullback Patrick DiMarco in the third quarter to key a 16–10 victory over 4th-ranked Mississippi, which at the time was the highest-ranked opponent the Gamecocks had defeated in decades. He finished his redshirt sophomore season as the first South Carolina quarterback to start every game since Dondrial Pinkins six years earlier, and he was second in the SEC in passing yards behind Ryan Mallett of Arkansas. The promise was evident, and he still had two more seasons to play.

The challenges, though, were not over, and they came to a head in the fourth game of Garcia's redshirt junior season against Auburn. Garcia had enjoyed an effective night passing the ball, throwing for a season-high 235 yards and three touchdowns. But a pair of fumbles committed while trying to run for extra yardage were too much for the Ball Coach, and Garcia was yanked with six minutes to play and the Gamecocks down eight. "When it came to Spurrier and Garcia, the leash was always short," recalled Travis Haney, who covered the 2010 season for the *Post and Courier* of Charleston, South Carolina. Even so, the former Gamecocks beat writer recalls being "totally shocked" when Spurrier pulled his starter out of the Auburn game.

"As much as they might have liked Shaw's potential, and for good reason, Garcia had not been bad at all in that game," Haney added. "I think Spurrier was sometimes too emotional when it came to Garcia, but I'm sure plenty of other Spurrier quarterbacks would say he was the same way with them, too. You think about it now, and maybe the Gamecocks win that game if Garcia stays in. I mean, hell, the box score for the Auburn game actually looks better than the Alabama game that's thought of as his masterpiece. It's crazy how close they were in that one."

But on the morning after the Auburn meltdown, an upset of the defending national champions seemed very far away, even though the Gamecocks had the luxury of two weeks to prepare. "I don't know what we'll do," Spurrier said, when asked about his starting quarterback situation. More than Garcia's performance against the Tigers, Spurrier seemed concerned about the way the quarterback scrambled—with his head down, which the Head Ball Coach believed made him more vulnerable to not just fumbles, but also injury. "I think he closes his eyes and he dives in there," Spurrier said. "That's a recipe for disaster. I'm really concerned about his health as we proceed. Something bad could happen."

With Garcia, it was always something. Later, it was reported that Spurrier hadn't notified Garcia he had been pulled from the Auburn game—the quarterback found out when he saw his backup Shaw jogging in. But days later, after a review of Garcia's play at Auburn and an understanding that the quarterback couldn't scramble into hits that would knock the ball loose, Spurrier announced that Garcia would indeed retain his starting role against Alabama. And then suddenly, the spotlight on the Gamecocks got even bigger: CBS placed the game in its marquee 3:30 p.m. television slot, and ESPN announced its popular *College GameDay* program was coming to Columbia, where it would originate from the Horseshoe for the showdown between No. 19 South Carolina and the top-ranked Crimson Tide.

With the drama over a starting quarterback settled—for the time being—attention turned to Alabama, which was a touchdown favorite over the Gamecocks. That spread existed for good reason, given that Alabama had throttled No. 7 Florida, 31–6, the weekend before, while South Carolina's defense had been picked apart by Auburn in its most recent outing. And yet, in Columbia, there was the sneaking suspicion that South Carolina could give Alabama a game. The Gamecocks had done just that the last time they had hosted the nation's No. 1 team, the season before against Florida— South Carolina had the lead and the ball in the fourth quarter, only to lose both when Garcia ad-libbed into an interception returned for a touchdown that swung the momentum in the Gators' 24–14 victory.

And two weeks earlier, Alabama had come out flat at Arkansas, falling behind 20–7 before rallying to win. "They haven't just steamrolled everyone,"

Spurrier pointed out. Writing in *The State* newspaper of Columbia, columnist Ron Morris opined that "everything is in place for USC to defeat Alabama at Williams-Brice Stadium." That sentiment, though, didn't seem very believable outside the boundaries of the Palmetto State. When Haney appeared on Paul Finebaum's syndicated radio program—then based out of Birmingham, Alabama—and mentioned that he thought the Gamecocks had a chance, the host started laughing.

"He thought I was just being some local homer guy, but I believed it'd be close," Haney recalled. "They'd already beaten Georgia, they played well enough to be competitive at Auburn, they were coming off a bye. They'd played a 20–6 game the previous year in Tuscaloosa, and I thought having [tailback] Marcus Lattimore as a freshman could give them an edge, finally giving them a chance to run the ball against 'Bama. I didn't see the game playing out the way that it did, but I thought they'd have a chance in the fourth quarter, sort of like the Auburn game."

In reality, it would be nothing like the Auburn game. It would be complete domination, with the Gamecocks running out to a 21–3 lead and never looking back, stunning both the college football nation and a joyous home stadium. "It's not like we just lost," Alabama head coach Nick Saban said

Despite memorable moments that included South Carolina's greatest regular-season victory—a triumph over No. 1 Alabama in 2010—quarterback Stephen Garcia was ultimately dismissed from the squad by athletic director Eric Hyman. *Courtesy of the* Post and Courier, *Charleston, S.C.*

afterward. "They beat us. They out-executed us. They played better than we played. They played with more intensity." And the catalyst to all of it was Garcia, whose two early touchdown passes to future NFL star Alshon Jeffery set the tone. For one day, at least, the full potential of South Carolina with Garcia on his game was evident for all to see.

"I think everyone—including Spurrier—knew that he was totally capable of playing like that every week," Haney said. "That was what frustrated fans and the staff most. He was an incredibly talented guy who couldn't take the next steps for a handful of reasons. He was a good kid, smart kid—but also just really immature, something I think he'd admit now. I mean, even in the middle of this 'perfect' game, the second half starts with him making this really bizarre play of picking up a fumble and then firing it backward into the goal post for a safety. There was just never going to be anything completely smooth with him running the operation. You accepted that, I think, because he still gave you the best shot to win."

Just over a month later, Garcia and the Gamecocks would turn in another near-flawless effort at Florida, where they clinched the program's first SEC East title and secured a spot in the league's championship game. Two weeks after that, Garcia threw two touchdown passes as South Carolina won the second of what would become five straight games over rival Clemson. With Garcia at the helm, the Gamecocks had finally reached the peak they had long been climbing toward—and then they tumbled off it.

First came a 56–17 humbling in the SEC title game—not against McElroy and Alabama, but old nemesis Auburn, which was on its way to the national championship. Then there was the Chick-fil-A Bowl, and three Garcia interceptions in a 26–17 loss to a Florida State team playing a backup quarterback for most of the game. Then, that following March, came the news that Garcia had once again been suspended—this time for the first week of spring practice, due to conduct violations stemming from the bowl game. In April came yet another suspension, this one for his behavior during an SEC leadership meeting. In October, midway through a season in which the Gamecocks had started 5-1 despite inconsistency at the quarterback position, Garcia was dismissed for good—not by Spurrier but by athletic director Eric Hyman.

After weathering five suspensions over the course of his time in Columbia, the final blow for Garcia was failing a random substance test that indicated alcohol use, *The State* reported. A tumultuous and star-crossed career had come to a sudden end. Earlier that season, Garcia had again been benched—this time after throwing his ninth interception, most in the country to that point—giving way to Shaw, who took his first real steps toward what would become a legendary stint behind center. Garcia left his imprint all over South Carolina's record book, finishing third in school history in passing yards and touchdowns and at the time tied with Steve Taneyhill for second in wins. And he had played a major role in some of the biggest victories of the Spurrier era, none bigger than that October day in 2010 when his near-perfect afternoon helped the Gamecocks take down the mighty Crimson Tide. For all the drama that surrounded him in Columbia, it remains the one, signature moment fans best remember from his too-brief stint wearing garnet and black.

"I think everyone remembers him pretty warmly considering how it ended. And maybe Shaw being so damn good helps with that, softening the blow," Haney said. "Stephen embodied all the potential in the world, but the staff and Stephen himself couldn't ever reach the potential on a consistent basis. That's kind of what made that Alabama game stand out—for one Saturday, this was as close as he was ever going to get."

12

MAKING OF A MIRACLE

The weekend before he had suffered a partial tear of a ligament in his left knee, an injury that had kept him out of practice and was expected to take weeks to heal. Over the previous two days he had been wracked with nausea and vomiting, to the point that when the team charter touched down in Columbia, Missouri, the training staff had him ride to the hotel in the back seat of the police escort rather than on the bus with everyone else.

Indeed, it had been a rough week for Connor Shaw. So, in the visiting locker room beneath the University of Missouri's Faurot Field, before a critical game between two contenders for the SEC East title, South Carolina head coach Steve Spurrier approached his senior quarterback and told him he didn't have to dress out. Shaw had been sick, he hadn't practiced all week and backup Dylan Thompson—who had shined in a similar role against Clemson the season before—was a more than able substitute.

"I told him I had been voted by the team to be a captain earlier in the year during the summer," Shaw recalled, "and the least I could do was dress to do the coin flip at the 50-yard line."

That sense of loyalty to his teammates was why Shaw was in uniform rather than sweats on that October night in 2013. It also put him in position to handle much more than just the coin toss—midway through the third quarter, after seeing too much offensive ineptitude in a game South Carolina trailed 17–0, Spurrier flung down his play sheet, turned and locked eyes with

Shaw on the sideline. "I knew it was coming," the quarterback remembered. "He said, 'Connor, can you go?' I said, 'Yes, sir.' He said 'All right, go ahead. It's got to happen now.'"

What happened was a comeback for the ages, one of the greatest victories in Gamecocks football history, a storybook finish in which the injured Shaw came off the bench to rally South Carolina for a 27–24 triumph that was sealed in double overtime when Missouri kicker Andrew Baggett clanked a tying field-goal attempt off the upright. Few Gamecock victories rekindle such breathless magic as the "Miracle in Missouri," where Shaw found Nick Jones for the tying touchdown with forty-two seconds left, hit Bruce Ellington for an astounding 15-yard score on fourth down in the first overtime and cemented his legacy as one of the toughest and most successful players to ever wear the garnet and black.

But just getting to that point required its own struggle, given where Shaw and the Gamecocks had been one week before: at Neyland Stadium in Knoxville, Tennessee, where South Carolina had been roughed up by a mediocre Tennessee team playing its first season under new head coach Butch Jones. On that day, the Volunteers recorded their lone victory over a ranked opponent. The 23–21 loss to the Volunteers, decided on a field goal at the horn, would loom large in the SEC East race. But so would something else that occurred late in the fourth quarter—Shaw getting sandwiched between two members of Tennessee's defensive line, 351-pound tackle Daniel McCullers and 272-pound end Marlon Walls. The Gamecocks quarterback was helped off the field, had his left leg fitted in a brace that extended from his thigh to his ankle and hobbled to the locker room on crutches.

"He sort of got tackled on it, and it collapsed under him a little bit, he said," Spurrier told reporters after the game. "How serious, they'll have to wait and evaluate."

As a mobile quarterback who took his share of hits, Shaw had dealt with plenty of injuries over the course of his South Carolina career—but not to his knees. Watching the replay later, it was clear how his left knee had twisted under the weight of the two Tennessee defenders. The knee swelled up immediately, and the level of inflammation had everyone concerned. Shaw's primary worry was over a potential tear of the anterior cruciate knee ligament, an injury that would require surgery to repair and put Shaw out of action for the remainder of the season.

"Oh, 100 percent," said Shaw, who after stints in the NFL joined the staff of his alma mater as the Gamecocks' director of football student-athlete development. "I don't know what that feels like, but just from the action and the immediate sharp pain from it, I was praying it wasn't [an ACL]. But that was where my mind was at."

Word quickly spread that the injury wasn't as bad as initially feared. ESPN reported that an MRI performed on Shaw's left knee had shown no damaged ligaments, and Spurrier the next day referred to the injury rather innocuously as a knee sprain. "Connor Shaw is actually walking around a little bit," the Head Ball Coach told reporters on his Sunday conference call. "They're calling it a knee sprain. No surgery or anything. I'm not sure what his status will be later in the week. He's obviously not practicing the first two, three days. I would think he would be able to come back. I'm sort of doubtful he'll be ready to do much this week."

It was a statement that left plenty to the imagination as far as Shaw's status for the following week's game at No. 5 Missouri, which—due to the loss at Tennessee—the Gamecocks almost certainly had to win to remain in the race for the SEC East championship. Shaw's actual injury, he says now, was a Grade 2 sprain of his left lateral collateral ligament, which helps to keep the knee stable. A Grade 2 diagnosis means there are tears within the ligament, although it is not completely torn, and simply walking can lead to the knee occasionally giving out. The injury typically takes two to four weeks to heal, according to Harvard Medical School.

Indeed, Spurrier referenced a similar timeline in comments to reporters the Tuesday after the Tennessee game. "The trainers feel like in a couple of weeks, two to three weeks, he may be close to a hundred percent on that thing," the head coach said. On that same day, Spurrier named Thompson as the starter for the forthcoming contest at Missouri. Beat writer Ryan Wood of the *Post and Courier* in Charleston echoed the general consensus in his story for the following day's newspaper: "South Carolina quarterback Connor Shaw will return from a sprained knee at some point this season," he wrote, "but it won't be this week."

At least, that's how it seemed at the time. Shaw, meanwhile, was doing all that injured players can do: resting and going through rehabilitation. The day after he suffered the injury, he spent time primarily in the training room and watching film. Unable to practice that week, he sat in on meetings and did what he could to help Thompson get ready to start. As the week went on, he began to throw the football around a bit. At midweek, he had a brace put on his left leg, and the extra support gave him a boost of confidence. Watching practice, he put himself through "mental reps" to keep his decision-making sharp.

Lightly recruited by SEC teams, Connor Shaw evolved into South Carolina's most successful quarterback, amassing a 27-5 record as a starter that included a perfect 17-0 mark at home. He led the Gamecocks to three straight eleven-win seasons from 2011 to 2013. *Courtesy of the* Post and Courier, *Charleston, S.C.*

"I knew I was going to dress out," he recalled. "I still wanted to have the mindset that week that I was going to prepare like I was going to play. But I had the full intention of Dylan seeing it through."

And yet during South Carolina's team walk-through on the Friday before the Missouri game, Shaw felt good enough that "if I felt like I had to, I could go," he said. Even Spurrier had left open the possibility that his injured starter could "get in as a backup, we don't know." Such a comeback would hardly have been out of character for Shaw, who time and time again throughout his Gamecock career returned from injury sooner than anyone outside of the South Carolina locker room expected. Earlier in that 2013 season, he had left a game at Central Florida in the first quarter with a right shoulder sprain and was not expected to play the following week against Kentucky. Yet Shaw started against the Wildcats and was a crisp seventeen of twenty for 262 yards and a touchdown in a 35–28 victory.

"It was one of those situations where Shaw's availability didn't sound promising during the week, but then there's always the potential for gamesmanship, so you just don't know," Wood recalled. "The magnitude of that game—especially coming after a deflating letdown at Tennessee one week earlier—made me think in the very back recesses of my mind there was a chance Shaw could play. This was supposed to be a special season for South Carolina, and without Shaw, a week after the train sort of ran off the rails, it felt like the Gamecocks could be led to the slaughter. Dylan Thompson was seen as a capable backup, a pocket quarterback who could throw, but he didn't have Shaw's playmaking or experience. So the smart bet was on Shaw not playing, but I thought it was possible, if only because South Carolina absolutely needed this game in order to have the season it expected. Then, of course, Thompson got the start, and it seemed like that settled it."

But Shaw's knee, as it turned out, wasn't his only issue. He began vomiting on the flight to Missouri, and trainers were concerned enough about his condition that he rode to the hotel in the back of the police escort. "They kind of kept me quarantined," he recalled. That night and the next morning, he participated in no team meetings or activities, remaining in his hotel room receiving intravenous fluids. The illness—which Shaw guesses was the flu—stuck with him for days after the Missouri game, even forcing him to sit out practice on the Monday of the following week. "It just really knocked me out," Shaw said.

No wonder, then, that Spurrier gave him the option of watching the game in street clothes, an offer Shaw declined out of loyalty to teammates who had chosen him captain. On the sideline, he stuck close to Spurrier, so he could follow the head coach's decision-making process and play-calling. And he had an up-close view of the wretched series of events that put the Gamecocks in a 17–0 hole at halftime: two opening possessions that went three-and-out and gained a combined 7 yards, a missed 40-yard field-goal attempt, a slew of turnovers that included a fumble by running back Mike Davis at the Missouri 2 and a failed fourth-down conversion attempt at the Missouri 34. South Carolina, ranked No. 11 in the AP Top 25 before the Tennessee game, appeared well on its way to a second consecutive loss to an SEC East opponent.

The Gamecocks had full faith in Thompson, given how South Carolina's backup quarterback had excelled in similar situations before. The previous season, Thompson had started in place of an injured Shaw and thrown three touchdowns in a 27–17 victory at Clemson. Weeks later, in a 33–28 Outback

Bowl victory over Michigan better known for Jadeveon Clowney's helmet-popping hit on Wolverines running back Vincent Smith, Thompson tossed the winning touchdown pass to Ellington with eleven seconds remaining. Earlier in the 2013 season against Central Florida, he had again relieved an injured Shaw to engineer a 28–25 victory over a Knights team that would go on to finish 12-1 and win the Fiesta Bowl.

But on this night against a Missouri squad that presented one of the nation's best defenses, nothing was working. Midway through the third quarter, Spurrier had seen enough. Entering the game down 17–0, Shaw tried to keep it simple. "You're not going to win this in one series," he remembers telling himself, "so just move the sticks."

Up in the Faurot Field press box, Wood remembers thinking, if Shaw's capable of playing, then why didn't he start? "Because at the time he enters the game, this game is over. It's clearly too late, right?" he said. "No way Connor Shaw, Superman or Jesus Christ is bringing them back from down 17–0 in the fourth quarter on the road against an undefeated Missouri team, which also happened to be led by a great defense. And keep in mind, South Carolina looked mostly lifeless before Shaw walked onto the field. So to me it seemed like a pretty big mistake on both ends: not starting Shaw when he could have played, and choosing to insert him only after the game was practically over."

Once he entered the game, Shaw's adrenaline was pumping, initially eclipsing any concerns over his left knee. But in live action, a quarterback renowned for his scrambling ability quickly realized that he was less mobile than usual. "There were definitely some things that I couldn't do that I could normally do," he recalled. "I think [the knee injury] forced me to stay in the pocket a little bit. You could definitely tell that I was a little bit ginger on that left side. But in those moments, you don't really quite feel the pain. It was that Sunday morning when the pain started to set in."

For those watching on television back home in the Palmetto State, it didn't look painful—it looked like magic, as the Gamecocks clawed their way back into the game behind one dramatic moment after another. Entering the fourth quarter, South Carolina trailed 17–0 and faced a fourth-and-4. Shaw converted that with a 10-yard strike to Ellington, later found Davis for 19 yards to convert a third-and-19 and connected with Ellington again to get the Gamecocks on the board. After an Elliott Fry field goal, a 2-yard strike to Jones with 42 seconds remaining sent the game into overtime. There, the heroics continued in the extra period, when Shaw found Ellington in the corner of the end zone for an improbable tying touchdown on fourth-and-goal from the Missouri 15-yard-line.

Famous for his toughness, quarterback Connor Shaw overcame both a knee injury and pregame illness to rally South Carolina from a 17-point deficit to an overtime victory at fifth-ranked Missouri in 2013. *Courtesy of the* Post and Courier, *Charleston, S.C.*

Even Spurrier seemed a little stunned by it all. "I thought we were dead," he told reporters afterward.

Like most beat writers facing a tight deadline for a night game, Wood had already begun writing his story for the following day's newspaper, believing the outcome of the contest had been decided. South Carolina's first touchdown, coming early in the fourth quarter, initially seemed only to narrow the Gamecocks' inevitable margin of defeat. As Shaw and South Carolina executed one miracle play after another, the level of incredulity among those watching from the press box kept rising, and what had once been a one-sided game was suddenly headed into overtime.

"This game was out of hand, and South Carolina finally getting on the scoreboard early in the fourth quarter didn't change that fact," recalled Wood, who left the Charleston paper in 2014 to cover the NFL's Green Bay Packers. "So the mental progression was basically, they aren't winning, they can't win, no way they're pulling this off, wait a second they have a real chance to tie here, holy blankety-blank this game is actually heading to overtime? I mean, how is that even possible? It was a magical night for the program, and a very different feeling for the other Columbia."

To Shaw, so much of that night remains a blur. He remembers trying to be patient and start with just getting first downs. He remembers being more limited in the pocket than normal. He remembers remaining all business following the fourth-down overtime strike to Ellington, even though "the sideline was geeked up after that," he said. And after Fry connected on a 40-yard field goal in double overtime to give the Gamecocks their first lead of the game, he remembers watching Baggett clank his attempt at a tying kick from 24 yards out off the left upright and running directly toward the Mayor's Cup that the two SEC teams from cities named Columbia vie for each season.

"I just made a beeline for that thing," Shaw recalled. "I grabbed it, and went right to where the families and the people who had traveled from South Carolina were, and started beating my chest. It was just an incredible moment."

It was made even more so by the week that had preceded it, seven days dominated by questions over not just Shaw's health but also the direction of a South Carolina football program that had won eleven games two seasons running and was bidding to remain among the nation's elite. The Miracle in Missouri was the beginning of a season-ending six-game win streak, one that included a fifth straight victory over rival Clemson and saw Shaw cap his career with a magnificent performance in the Capital One Bowl, where he accounted for four touchdowns and nearly 400 yards of offense in a win over Wisconsin. The Gamecocks won eleven games for a third straight season and finished No. 4 in the final AP poll, unprecedented accomplishments that would not have been possible if not for one magical night at Faurot Field.

And it marked a personal vindication of sorts for Shaw, who, despite his accomplishments at South Carolina—he would finish a program-best 27-5 as a starter and a perfect 17-0 at Williams-Brice Stadium—felt like he needed a signature road victory over a highly ranked opponent. The Gamecocks had lost a shootout at No. 11 Georgia earlier in that 2013 season and the previous year had been nipped at No. 9 LSU and blown out at No. 3 Florida. After engineering the Miracle at Missouri, his legacy was complete.

"It was a personal goal of mine, and really necessary, for us to go play well on the road," Shaw recalled. "So it was a big confidence-booster for me, and one of those defining moments for our program."

13

From Spurrier to Muschamp

The thought first entered Steve Spurrier's head during the fourth game of the season, a slog past a terrible Central Florida team that would go winless on the year. The Gamecocks had trailed at halftime against one of the worst programs in college football's top division, and not even a second-half surge and a 31–14 victory were enough to inspire confidence from South Carolina's head coach. The Gamecocks were on their third starting quarterback, changes to shore up the defense weren't working as well as intended and signs were beginning to point toward the unthinkable: a losing record less than two years after finishing as the No. 4 team in the country.

The Head Ball Coach had never suffered a losing record in all his years overseeing college programs. To Spurrier, that fact was a point of pride—and the reason he had been so excited the previous season over a victory in the seemingly meaningless Independence Bowl, which allowed his Gamecocks to finish 7-6 rather than 6-7 and keep his run of winning seasons intact. But four games into the 2015 campaign, it was difficult to envision a similar salvage operation. South Carolina stood 2-2 but had experienced a precipitous drop in the talent level on its roster and faced a gauntlet of difficult games to come.

So the day after that struggle against Central Florida, the most successful football coach in South Carolina history called athletic director Ray Tanner and first raised the possibility of stepping down. "I'm going to try to get through this season, but I sense that this is about it for me. I just sense it's it," the seventy-year-old Spurrier told Tanner, who had won two national titles as South Carolina's baseball coach before moving into the AD role. "Central Florida, it was a struggle against those guys. I don't know if I need to continue having these kinds of struggles."

There would be more struggles ahead. The Gamecocks traveled to Missouri the following week and showed none of Spurrier's trademark offensive pizzazz in a 24–10 loss. Then there was a 45–24 rout at LSU in a game moved to Baton Rouge from Columbia due to the aftermath of historic flooding in the Palmetto State. In a very short time, the program had slipped in terms of recruiting, evident in the large number of current and former walk-ons the Gamecocks were being forced to employ. And now Spurrier himself was showing the strain in the form of uncharacteristically terse and bleak answers in press conferences, where he usually dazzled.

The Sunday after the LSU loss, Spurrier and Tanner met for ninety minutes in the football office at Williams-Brice Stadium and talked about the head coach's possible resignation. Later that same day, the two men spoke again by phone. Spurrier slept on it and Monday morning called Tanner to tell the athletic director he planned to resign immediately. Later that Monday, Tanner and university president Harris Pastides met with Spurrier in person and urged him to at least finish the season. But "he had made up his mind," Pastides said, and the Head Ball Coach planned to break the news to his team in a meeting that evening.

"When something is inevitable, I believe you do it right then," Spurrier said. "You don't wait a week, you don't wait two weeks. This has to happen. Let's do it, let's do it, let's get started in a new direction."

Soon after Spurrier informed his team, word of his resignation began to leak to the media, helped in part by social media posts made by current and former Gamecock players thanking their now-former head coach. By 10:00 p.m. that Monday, anyone near a phone, laptop or television had heard the news. With another game looming in just five days, things happened quickly: former offensive line coach Shawn Elliott was named interim head coach for the remainder of the season, and Spurrier's resignation—he didn't want to call it a retirement, and true to his word he'd be back to coach in a short-lived pro league in 2019—was made official in a press conference at Williams-Brice Stadium the following day.

"Somehow or another, we've slid," said Spurrier, who had led the Gamecocks to heights they'd never before experienced, including five straight wins over rival Clemson and three consecutive eleven-win seasons.

"And it's my fault. I'm responsible, I'm the head coach. And it's time for me to sort of get out of the way and let somebody else have a go at it."

From that point on, South Carolina proceeded on two tracks: trying to finish a football season and search for a new head football coach, all at the same time. Both processes would prove arduous. On the field, the young and high-energy Elliott made changes in an attempt to boost morale, like allowing music to be played during practice and unveiling a new, alternate helmet for one game. But after an emotional victory over Vanderbilt the first weekend following Spurrier's resignation, the same depth and talent issues that had dogged the Gamecocks all season took hold once again. South Carolina finished the campaign with five straight defeats, and though many of them were competitive, an embarrassing home loss to lower-level The Citadel effectively scuttled any hopes Elliott had of securing the job full-time.

Meanwhile, South Carolina had quickly zeroed in on a lead candidate to replace Spurrier: Tom Herman, the forty-year-old former offensive coordinator at Ohio State who had emerged as the hottest young coach in the country at unbeaten Houston, which would ultimately finish that 2015 season 13-1. The Gamecocks had plenty to offer, including a faithful fan base, improving facilities and money from their lucrative membership in the SEC. For all the program's shortcomings at present, very recently it had ranked among the best in the nation, so the potential was clearly there. Herman returned the interest. According to *USA Today*, the two sides were proceeding so seamlessly toward an agreement that South Carolina effectively shut down its search process. The Gamecocks had their man.

Until they didn't. The 23–22 loss to The Citadel, which played at a lower rung on the NCAA ladder, made the Gamecocks look like a program with a long, difficult rebuilding job ahead of them. Not only did the defeat nix any hopes Elliott had of getting the job, but it also led Herman to change his mind and stay in Houston. Two weeks later, he reached an agreement on a contract extension with the Cougars that boosted his annual pay to around $3 million. One year later, he was hired as head coach at Texas.

South Carolina, meanwhile, was suddenly looking around for other options. The Gamecocks made a play for Alabama defensive coordinator Kirby Smart, only to suffer the bad timing of seeing his alma mater, Georgia, part ways with coach Mark Richt. Smart was Georgia's "only choice," and South Carolina lost out on its No. 2 candidate. In media reports, one coach after another began to crop up in connection with the Gamecocks opening—Rich Rodriguez at Arizona, Willie Taggart at South

Florida, Oklahoma offensive coordinator Lincoln Riley, Sonny Dykes at Cal—though not all of them would prove to be legitimate candidates. On November 30, Will Muschamp's name first arose in a Fox Sports report that mentioned that the former Florida head coach and current Auburn defensive coordinator was receiving "some consideration" for the position.

Gamecocks fans were left in a state of high anxiety over seeing one job after another filled while theirs remained vacant. After having consecutive Hall of Fame coaches in Lou Holtz and Spurrier, there was the belief—undeterred by the travails of the just-completed season—that the South Carolina program had reached such a level that it could attract another elite name. The Herman saga, not known in full until *USA Today* reported it three months later, had unfolded largely behind the scenes. The idea that the Gamecocks were pursuing Muschamp—who had been unable to win consistently at Florida, one of the top programs in the nation, and been fired after an overtime loss to the Gamecocks in 2014— was a galling prospect to many fans, to say the least.

Yet the task of proving himself was nothing new to Muschamp, who prior to his stint at Florida had been every bit the hot young coaching prospect that Herman was at the time. Prior to taking the Florida job, Muschamp

Although the Gamecocks had initially explored other candidates, a relationship with athletic director Ray Tanner helped Will Muschamp earn the job of succeeding Steve Spurrier as South Carolina's head coach in 2015. *Courtesy of the* Post and Courier, *Charleston, S.C.*

had been named "head coach in waiting" at Texas, where he served as defensive coordinator under Mack Brown. Even after being fired as Florida's head coach, he was quickly snapped up as Auburn's defensive coordinator, retaining his reputation as one of the foremost defensive minds in the sport. And South Carolina's rebuilding job would have to begin on defense, a fact made clear by the shortcomings of Spurrier's final two seasons.

So, Muschamp was nothing if not dogged, a trait he would display again and again as a player and a coach. In a frame behind his desk in his office, Muschamp kept an odd memento: a seventeen-inch metal rod that had been implanted in his lower right leg to repair a compound fracture suffered when he collided with a teammate while playing for his high school baseball team. Once a highly recruited football player, he went through months of rehabilitation and saw almost all of his college scholarship offers dry up. Muschamp walked on at Georgia, where he ultimately earned a scholarship and enjoyed a solid career as a safety. Following his dismissal at Florida, where he went 28-21 in four years, he was determined to again become a head coach in the SEC. He saw his chance at South Carolina and went after it hard, reaching out to Pastides and Gamecock great Marcus Lattimore in an attempt to bolster his position with the school.

Muschamp had something else going for him as well: a relationship with Tanner, which had developed the previous year during a coach-to-coach conversation between the two men—likely at the SEC's annual spring meetings—while Muschamp still worked at Florida. "It stuck with me, the conversation and the tone," Tanner said later. "There was a bond." Unable to nail down a new head coach, Tanner remembered that talk. He texted Muschamp, and when the coach arrived for his interview, the two chatted from early evening until 1:00 a.m. After sleeping for a few hours, Tanner called Muschamp to talk further. He received strong feedback from officials at Florida, who had developed a fondness for Muschamp and the manner in which he had cleaned up the Gators' program, even though things didn't go as well as anticipated on the field.

It was all good enough for Tanner, and the deal was done. Of the thirteen programs in the NCAA's top five conferences that had been looking for a head coach that season, South Carolina would be the last to fill its position. Among the Gamecocks fan base, the hire was polarizing to say the least, although Muschamp won over some people with an enthusiastic introductory press conference and immediate examples of his famed recruiting acumen. Muschamp was out meeting with recruits the same day he was hired, in the same suit in which he had been introduced to the media, and quickly succeeded in flipping one Columbia high school standout from Louisville to South Carolina.

Muschamp's results on the field would be initially hopeful—he took South Carolina to bowl games in each of his first three seasons—before concerns arose in 2019 over an injury-plagued 4-8 record and a revolving door of offensive coordinators who struggled to get the Gamecocks' attack to click. But his relentless style meshed with a program trying to make headway among rival Clemson and the powers in the SEC, and his ability to build personal relationships was evident both in his bonds with players and the improved connections he quickly established with high school coaches in the state.

So, there was indeed optimism on that December day in 2015, when the Head Ball Coach gave way to a younger successor whose fiery sideline demeanor earned him the nickname "Coach Boom." The search had taken fifty-four days and made several unexpected turns along the way, but South Carolina had finally chosen the football coach who would lead the Gamecocks into the post-Spurrier era. "We got to the place we needed to," Tanner said when Muschamp was officially introduced at Williams-Brice Stadium, "with the right man."

SOURCES

1. A Riotous Mood

Atlanta Constitution. "Morning Game Was Jonah to Clemson in Columbia."
    October 31, 1902.

Biographical Directory of the United States Congress. Washington, D.C.: U.S.
    Government Printing Office.

Clemson University. Catalogue, 1902–03.

Evening Post (Charleston, SC). "Foot Ball in the Colleges." November 26,
    1900.

Hollis, Daniel Walker. *University of South Carolina*. Volume II. Columbia:
    University of South Carolina Press, 1951.

McCormick, Jacob. "Outbreak of a Rivalry: The Carolina-Clemson Riot
    of 1902." Lecture, Columbia Historic Foundation, November 16, 2002.

National Park Service, Thomas Sumter biography. www.nps.gov.

Pierce, Robert A. "Clemson at 100 Is a 'Cow College' No Longer." *The State*
    (Columbia, SC), April 17, 1988.

Schwartz, Evan Scott. "How South Carolina Got Its Nickname." *Sports
    Illustrated*, November 11, 2014.

Spear, Bob. "The S.C. Rivalry that Almost Wasn't." *The State*, November
    17, 2002.

The State. "They've Buried the Hatchet." November 1, 1902.

———. "The Trouble Over the Transparency." November 2, 1902.

2. Banned

Hollis, Daniel Walker. *University of South Carolina*. Volume II. Columbia: University of South Carolina Press, 1951.

Miller, John J. *The Big Scrum: How Teddy Roosevelt Saved Football*. New York: Harper Perennial, 2012.

The State. "Carolina Trustees Forbid Football." January 14, 1906.

———. "Football Again at Carolina." October 31, 1907.

———. "Football Again for University." October 30, 1907.

———. "Football Squads Working into Form." October 5, 1907.

———. "Pigskin Season Will Be on Soon." September 28, 1907.

———. "The Southern Colleges." October 14, 1907.

———. "Want Football at University." October 29, 1097.

Zezima, Katie. "How Teddy Roosevelt Helped Save Football." *Washington Post*, May 29, 2014.

3. Victory and War

Associated Press. "Upstate Team Given Surprise." *Evening Post*, October 24, 1941.

Ballantine, Red. "Just Talking Sports." *The State*, November 1, 1942.

Fennell, Abe. "Carolina Scores Startling Upset over Clemson in Classic." *The State*, October 24, 1941.

Gamecocks Online. "The First Gamecock Football AP All-American: Lou Sossamon." September 22, 2015.

Gardner, Ian, and Roger Day. *Tonight We Die as Men*. Oxford, UK: Osprey Publishing, 2009.

Griffin, John Chandler. *The First Hundred Years*. Atlanta, GA: Longstreet Press, 1992.

Haney, Travis. "Living Legends: USC's Oldest Former Football Players Recall Gamecocks' Rich History." *Post and Courier* (Charleston, SC), July 23, 2011.

Hitt, E.M., Jr. "Gamecocks Strike Early and Often to Beat Clemson." *News and Courier* (Charleston, SC), October 24, 1941.

Jones, Wilbur D. Jr. *Football! Navy! War! How Military Lend-Lease Players Saved the College Game and Helped Win World War II*. Jefferson, NC: McFarland, 2009.

Mather, Victor. "The Best College Football Team You've Probably Never Heard Of." *New York Times*, August 21, 2017.

Penland, Jake. "Looking Out from the Press Box with Jake Penland." *The State*, June 28, 1942.

———. "Stan Stasica Will Be Drafted into Army August 1." *The State*, July 17, 1942.

The Record (Columbia, SC). "Carolina Loses Guard Doyle Norman." September 2, 1942.

———. "Slim Squad Will Report to Enright." August 27, 1942.

———. "Stasica Signs with Clippers." March 17, 1947.

Smith, Banjo. "On Second Thought.…" *The Record*, August 21, 1942.

———. "On Second Thought.…" *The Record*, September 2, 1942.

Thompson, Jimmie. "The Crow's Nest." *The State*, April 5, 1943.

4. Lone Star Stunner

Benson, Ray. "Longhorns Favored Over Gamecocks." *The State*, October 5, 1957.

———. "Gamecocks Live Up to Their Names." *The State*, October 7, 1957.

———. "Gamecocks Rally, Beat Texas 27–21." *The State*, October 6, 1957.

Donehue, Doug. "Topsy-turvy Football Weekend Left Plenty of Raised Eyebrows." *News and Courier*, October 8, 1957.

Griffin, John Chandler. *The First Hundred Years*. Atlanta, GA: Longstreet Press, 1992.

Heck, Kyle. "Dixon: I Love the University of South Carolina and I Always Have." *Spurs and Feathers*, November 15, 2015.

Klingaman, Mike. "Alex Hawkins, Irreverent, Rugged Captain Who? of 1960s Colts, Dies at Age 80." *Baltimore Sun*, September 13, 2017.

News and Courier. "Gamecocks' Amazing Rally Tramples Longhorns 27–21." October 6, 1957.

———. "Sophmoritis Wrecked Texans." *News and Courier*, October 7, 1957.

———. "South Carolina's Win One of Top U.S. Upsets." *The State*, October 7, 1957.

Penland, Jake. "In the Press Box with Jake Penland." *The State*, October 8, 1957.

Scoppe, Rick, and Charlie Bennett. *Game of My Life: Memorable Stories of Gamecocks Football*. New York: Sports Publishing, 2007.

Sports Illustrated. "Atlantic Coast Conference." September 23, 1957.

5. Black Friday

Barker, Barbara. "NFL's Decision to Play Two Days after JFK's Murder Was Big Mistake," *Newsday*, November 21, 2013.

Blackman, Sam, and Tim Bourret. "November 22, 1963." Football game program feature. www.clemsontigers.com.

Gavin, Michael. *Sports in the Aftermath of Tragedy: From Kennedy to Katrina.* Lanham, MD: Scarecrow Press, 2013.

Grose, Philip. "It Just Wasn't Big Thursday," *The State*, November 29, 1963.

Helms, Herman. "Clemson Rally Nips Spunky Gamecocks." *The State*, November 29, 1963.

———. "South Carolina–Clemson Football Classic Postponed Until Thanksgiving Afternoon." *The State*, November 23, 1963.

Hunter, Jim. "'I Couldn't Have Asked for More.'" *The State*, November 29, 1963.

———. "3,000 Students Show Support for Gamecocks." *The State*, November 22, 1963.

John F. Kennedy Presidential Library and Museum. "November 22, 1963: Death of a President."

Penland, Jake. Column. *The State*, November 24, 1963.

Pierce, Charles. "Black Sunday: The NFL Plays after JFK's Assassination." *Sports Illustrated*, November 24, 2003.

Price, Tom. *Tales from the Gamecocks' Roost*. New York: Sports Publishing, 2001.

Shutt, Steve. "50 Years Ago Today: Deacons and N.C. State Played Following JFK Assassination." godeacs.com, November 22, 2013.

The State. "The Saddest Big Thursday." November 29, 1963.

6. Cardiac Champions

Gillespie, Bob. "The 1969 Gamecocks: The One. The Only." *The State*, March 14, 2015.

Helms, Herman. "Another Gamecock Thrill Show Spills Spunky UNC." *The State*, September 28, 1969.

———. "Gamecocks Meet Challenge, Sweep 75 Yards in Dying Moments to Knock off Duke, 27–20." *The State*, September 21, 1969.

———. "Gamecocks Shoot for 2nd ACC Win Tonight against Tar Heels." *The State*, September 27, 1969.

———. "Long Mitchell, Harris Kick Returns Trigger Gamecocks to 21–16 Triumph over State." *The State*, October 12, 1969.

————. "One of Those Tight Stomach Games." *The State*, October 13, 1969.

————. "'69 Gamecocks Should Be Dietzel's Best." *The State*, September 17, 1969.

————. "South Carolina, Duke, 'Somewhat Similar.'" *The State*, September 17, 1969.

————. "There Is Some Reason for Hope." *The State*, September 14, 1969.

————. "Title Hopes On Line in State-USC Clash." *The State*, October 11, 1969.

————. "USC Gambled, Lived to Talk About It." *The State*, September 22, 1969.

————. "USC to Resign from ACC August 15." *The State*, March 30, 1971.

Joyce, Pat. "Watson Couldn't Believe the Loss." *News and Courier*, December 31, 1969.

Martin, Harold. "Gamecocks' Ace Receiver Almost Missed Opportunity." *The State*, September 17, 1969.

————. "Scrimmage Disappoints USC's Dietzel." *The State*, September 14, 1966.

Mitchell, Bill. "'Biggest Opening Game of Career,' Declares Dietzel." *The State*, September 21, 1969.

————. "'North Carolina Outplayed Us,' Declares Dietzel." *The State*, September 28, 1969.

Morris, George. "Before His Football Fame, World War II Shaped Paul Dietzel." *The Advocate* (Baton Rouge, LA), September 9, 2016.

News and Courier. "Mounties Down USC." December 31, 1969.

O'Neill, John V. "Carolina Fans Hail ACC Champions." *The Sate*, November 16, 1969.

Sanders, Jerry. "Half of USC's Season Is Over." *News and Courier*, November 16, 1969.

————. "South Carolina Clinches ACC Crown." *News and Courier*, November 16, 1969.

Suggs, Tommy. Interview, August 9, 2019.

7. The Birth of Williams-Brice

Adams, Frank. "USC Receives $3.5 Million from Estate." *The State*, January 3, 1971.

Biographical Directory of the United States Congress. Washington, D.C.: U.S. Government Printing Office.

Caraviello, David. "Gamecocks' Baseball Stadium Renamed in 10-Year, $7 Million Deal." *Post and Courier*, October 21, 2015.

Gillespie, Bob. "History Runs Deep: The Home of the Gamecocks Has as Many Stories to Tell as the Team Itself." *The State*, September 19, 2009.

Hare, Ken. "$4 Million of Donation for Stadium." *The State*, December 24. 1970.

————. "Part of Brice Funds to Go for Stadium." *The State*, May 19, 1971.

Kendall, Josh. "A History Lesson on Williams-Brice Stadium." *The State*, July 23, 2015.

New York Times. "Rep. L. Mendel Rivers Is Dead; Powerful Military Affairs Chief." December 29, 1970.

The State. "Carolina Stadium to Be Renamed for Benefactor." April 30, 1972.

————. "Name Change Was Bad." Letter to the Editor. June 2, 1972.

————. "Stadium Gets New Name." September 10, 1972.

————. "USC Officials Donors Decline to Comment on $5 Million Gift." December 25, 1970.

————. "Word Awaited on Gift." December 22, 1970.

Suggs, Tommy. Interview, August 9, 2019.

Sumter Item. "Despite Plant Closure, Sumter's Glass Half-full." June 30, 2004.

Tringali, Dot. "University to Honor Benefactor." *The Record*, January 11, 1971.

8. *What Could Have Been*

Caraviello, David. "Emotions Ran High Last Time USC Played Miami." *Post and Courier*, December 14, 2014.

Edwards, Brad. Interview, August 8, 2019.

Gillespie, Bob. "Edwards' TD Theft Gave Ford Flashback." *The Record*, November 23, 1987.

————. "Ellis Unable to Rally USC." *The Record*, December 7, 1987.

————. "Human Factor Is Thwarting USC Scoring." *The Record*, September 28, 1987.

————. "USC Signals Changing of Guard." *The Record*, November 23, 1987.

————. "USC's Loss Hauntingly Reminiscent." *The Record*, October 5, 1987.

Heffner, Teddy. "Miami Downs Pesky Gamecocks." *The State*, December 6, 1987.

Sapakoff, Gene. "Nebraska Spoils Gamecocks' Bid." *News and Courier*, October 4, 1987.

9. Steroids and Scandal

Chaikin, Tommy, with Rick Telander. "The Nightmare of Steroids." *Sports Illustrated*, October 23, 1988.

Cloninger, David. "Gamecocks Bringing Back 'Black Magic' with Throwback Uniforms from 1980s." *Post and Courier*, August 14, 2019.

———. "University of South Carolina Rebrands with 'Carolina' Logo." *Post and Courier*, September 1, 2018.

Cole, Bob. "Grand Jury to Study Ex-USC Player's Drug Claims." *The State*, October 20, 1988.

Gillespie, Bob. "Chaikin's Charges Raise New Questions." *The State*, October 21, 1988.

———. "Ex-Coach Details Steroid Talk with Morrison." *The State*, October 22, 1988.

———. Interview, February 12, 2019.

———. "Winning with Consequence." *The State*, November 9, 2003.

Gillespie, Bob, and Teddy Heffner. "Ex-USC Player Said Coaches Knew Steroids Used." *The State*, October 19, 1988.

Iacobelli, Pete. "USC Endured Steroid 'Nightmare.'" Associated Press, August 27, 2005.

Jenkins, Sally. "A South Carolina Scandal: Former Gamecock Football Player Chaikin Tries to Regroup After Disclosing Steroid Use." *Washington Post*, March 27, 1989.

Johnson, Dave. "South Carolina Football Program Weathers Storm." *Newport News (VA) Daily Press*, September 6, 1989.

Newton, David. Interview, July 22, 2019.

New York Times. "Acquittal in Steroid Trial." June 22, 1989.

———. "4 Ex-Football Aides Indicted in South Carolina Steroid Case." April 20, 1988.

———. "Sentences in Steroid Case." August 11, 1989.

Sapakoff, Gene. "More Player Spite Before the 1987 Game." *Post and Courier*, November 21, 2012.

———. "USC Players Savor Big Win." *News and Courier*, July 27, 1990.

Scoppe, Rick. "Morrison Looked Other Way, Report Says." Associated Press, February 22, 1990.

United Press International. "Former South Carolina Defensive Lineman Driven by Steroids." October 19, 1988.

10. The Real Thing

Cole, Bob. "Numbers Back Up Woods on Gamecocks' Youth." *The State*, October 11, 1992.

Gillespie, Bob. "Confidence Taneyhill's Most Visible Trait." *The State*, October 18, 1992.

Hartsell, Jeff. "Halloween Shockers: USC's Winning Streak, Vols' Loss Streak Hit 3." *Post and Courier*, November 1, 1992.

———. "USC 'Mutiny' Quelled." *Post and Courier*, October 14, 1992.

Hurt, Cecil. "Steve Taneyhill Is Likely to Pick Gamecocks over Crimson Tide." *Tuscaloosa (AL) News*, January 5, 1992.

Iacobelli, Pete. "Ex-Gamecocks Coach Remembers Turbulent 1992." Associated Press, October 3, 2002.

Jenkins, Sally. "Steve Taneyhill." *Sports Illustrated*, August 30, 1993.

Lang, Bob, and Jeff Hartsell. "Players at USC Take Vote Seeking Woods' Resignation." *Post and Courier*, October 13, 1992.

Newton, David. Interview, July 22, 2019.

———. "Uncertain Truce Holds at USC." *The State*, October 14, 1992.

———. "Woods Refuses Players' Demand He Step Down." *The State*, October 13, 1992.

Post and Courier. "Taneyhill to Start against Miss. State." October 16, 1992.

Sapakoff, Gene. "Gamecocks Tame Tigers." *Post and Courier*, November 22, 1992.

Taneyhill, Steve. Interview, July 25, 2019.

White, Neil. "Signing the Tiger Paw, Taneyhill Was Just Having Fun." *The State*, November 22, 2012.

11. Turning the Tide

Haney, Travis. "Elliott Rips Offensive Line's Effort." *Post and Courier*, September 30, 2010.

———. "Garcia Gets QB Nod for USC." *Post and Courier*, September 29, 2010.

———. Interview, July 13, 2019.

———. "Meltdown: Four Turnovers in Final Quarter Doom Gamecocks." *Post and Courier*, September 26, 2010.

———. "Prime Opportunity: No. 19 South Carolina Gets Rare Shot to Take Down a Top-Ranked Team." *Post and Courier*, October 6, 2010.

———. "Proving Ground: No. 10 Gamecocks Reap Benefits of Preparation, Now Look to Build on Success." *Post and Courier*, October 11, 2010.

———. "A Question at QB: Who Will Start for USC?" *Post and Courier*, September 27, 2010.

———. "South Carolina Upsets Defending Champion Alabama, Knocking Off a No. 1 Ranked-Team for the First Time." *Post and Courier*, October 10, 2010.

———. "USC in National Spotlight." *Post and Courier*, October 4, 2010.

———. "USC Looks to Improve Protection on Offense." *Post and Courier*, October 9, 2010.

Hoke, Josh. "Gamecocks Shake Off Gaffe." *The State*, October 10, 2010.

Kendall, Josh. "Curse Killers." *The State*, October 10, 2010.

———. "Garcia Remains Starter." *The State*, September 29, 2010.

———. "Garcia Suspended to Start Spring." *The State*, March 15, 2011.

———. "Garcia's Dives Cause Concern." *The State*, September 27, 2010.

———. "Garcia's Gone: Senior QB Dismissed for Failed Test." *The State*, October 12, 2011.

Morris, Ron. "Fate Hands USC an Afternoon to Remember." *The State*, October 10, 2010.

———. "Here Is Why South Carolina Will Beat No. 1 Alabama." *The State*, October 8, 2010.

Person, Joseph. "All Eyes Are on QB Position." *The State*, August 23, 2010.

———. "All Eyes on Gamecocks' No. 5." *The State*, September 25, 2008.

———. "Garcia Cleared for Early Return." *The State*, July 31, 2008.

———. "Garcia Goes with the Flow." *The State*, August 6, 2010.

———. "Garcia Gone till August—USC Puts Its Foot Down." *The State*, March 26, 2008.

———. "Garcia Ignores Call of Duty." *The State*, December 18, 2009.

———. "Spurrier Sticks to His Script." *The State*, May 11, 2010.

———. "3 Strikes: Is Garcia Out?" *The State*, March 25, 2008.

———. "Thrown for a Loss." *The State*, November 15, 2009.

Post and Courier. "Sky's the Limit for Gamecocks." Editorial, October 11, 2010.

Roberts, Alex. "Stephen Garcia: Tragic Rise and Fall of a South Carolina Gamecocks Quarterback." *Bleacher Report*, October 12, 2011.

Sapakoff, Gene. "Closer to the Vintage Spurrier." *Post and Courier*, September 26, 2010.

———. "Garcia's 'Best Game' Is His Redemption." *Post and Courier*, October 10, 2010.

———. "Is the SEC Overrated?" *Post and Courier*, October 6, 2010.

12. Making of a Miracle

Cloninger, David. "Limping in the East." *The State*, October 21, 2013.

———. "Shaw Has Sprain; No Ligament Damage." *The State*, October 20, 2013.

Kendall, Josh. "Painful Loss." *The State*, October 20, 2013.

———. "Shaw, Shank, Redemption." *The State*, October 27, 2013.

Shaw, Connor. Interview, June 27, 2019.

White, Neil. "Thompson Named Starter." *The State*, October 23, 2013.

Wood, Ryan. "Gamecocks Upended by Tennessee." *Post and Courier*, October 20, 2013.

———. Interview, July 9, 2019.

———. "Thompson Will Start against Missouri." *Post and Courier*, October 23, 2013.

13. From Spurrier to Muschamp

Caraviello, David. "All Signs at USC Point Toward Muschamp." *Post and Courier*, December 6, 2015.

———. "Bond Helped Produce USC's New Coach." *Post and Courier*, December 8, 2015.

———. "Head Ball Coach Stepping Down." *Post and Courier*, October 13, 2015.

———. "High School Injury Shaped Determined Nature of USC Football Coach Muschamp." *Post and Courier*, August 7, 2016.

———. "Spurrier Steps Down; Elliott Named Interim Coach at USC." *Post and Courier*, October 14, 2015.

———. "USC Could Be Battling Georgia for Head Coach." *Post and Courier*, December 1, 2015.

———. "USC to Talk with Riley, Muschamp." *Post and Courier*, December 4, 2015.

———. "USC's Tanner Stuck to Plan, Got 'Right Man.'" *Post and Courier*, December 8, 2015.

———. "Will Muschamp Finally Fixing Defensive Problems that Have Plagued South Carolina for Years." *SEC Country*, November 6, 2017.

Cloninger, David. "Muschamp Reaches Out to USC Ambassador." *The State*, December 5, 2015.

Griffin, Tim. "Muschamp to Take Over as Coach at Texas When Brown Retires." ESPN.com, November 18, 2008

Kendall, Josh. "Coach Boom: USC's Next Coach." *The State*, December 7, 2015.

———. "Reports: Smart Headed to Georgia." *The State*, December 2, 2015.

———. "Spurrier: 'It's Time to Get Out of the Way.'" *The State*, October 14, 2015.

———. "Spurrier Retiring Immediately." *The State*, October 13, 2015.

Wolken, Dan. "Will Muschamp Didn't Make It at Florida, Can He Turn South Carolina Around?" *USA Today*, February 14, 2016.

INDEX

A

ACC championship 57, 59, 62, 63, 64, 67

Alabama 63, 93, 99, 100, 103, 117

Applegate, Bill 33

Arkansas 86, 93, 102, 103

Arrowsmith, Dewitt 33

Attaway, Tommy 33

B

Baggett, Andrew 108, 114

Bass, Marvin 44, 45, 46, 48, 49, 51, 53

Benet, Christie Jr.
  attempts to defuse 1902 riot 16
  background 18
  easing of tensions in 1902 riot 20
  escalation of tensions in 1902 riot 16, 19

interaction with Clemson before 1902 riot 19

proposed arbitration in 1902 riot 19

role in 1902 riot 15

role with Gamecocks 21

tenure as head coach 23

Bethea, Ryan 74

Big Thursday 16, 30, 51

Bisaccia, Rich 93

Black Magic 86, 88

Blades, Brian 79

Blakeman, Clete 76

Blouin, Harvey 30, 33

board of trustees 22, 23, 24, 26, 27, 28, 61, 66, 68, 69, 94

Bradley, Bob 48

Brice, Martha Williams 64, 66, 72

Brice, Tom 64

Bryant, Bear 35

ABOUT THE AUTHOR

A lifetime resident of the Palmetto State and a graduate of the University of South Carolina's journalism school, David Caraviello twice covered the Gamecocks over a twenty-five-year career as a sportswriter that took him to every SEC stadium, numerous bowl games, both the men's and women's Final Four and too many barbecue joints to count. Unwilling to take on the easy assignments, his stints as Gamecocks beat writer included consecutive 1-10 and 0-11 football seasons under Brad Scott and Lou Holtz, as well as Steve Spurrier's abrupt resignation late on a Monday night. In between stretches reporting on the Gamecocks, Caraviello covered auto racing, emerging as one of the foremost editorial voices in the sport. The 2000 South Carolina Sports Writer of the Year, Caraviello has earned numerous other writing accolades and is a two-time recipient of the Russ Catlin Award, the highest honor in motorsports journalism. He lives near Charleston, South Carolina, with his wife, two children and two dogs.

Visit us at
www.historypress.com
....